The Goeben & the Breslau

The Goeben and *Breslau*

The Goeben & the Breslau

The Imperial German Navy in the
Mediterranean,1914

ILLUSTRATED

The Flight of the Goeben and Breslau
Sir A. Berkeley Milne

With Short Extracts from
Sir Julian S. Corbett, W. L. Wyllie and Others

LEONAUR

The Goeben & the Breslau
The Imperial German Navy in the Mediterranean, 1914
ILLUSTRATED
The Flight of the Goeben and Breslau
By Sir A. Berkeley Milne
With Short Extracts from Sir Julian S. Corbett, W. L. Wyllie and Others

FIRST EDITION

Leonaur is an imprint of Oakpast Ltd

Copyright in this form © 2019 Oakpast Ltd

ISBN: 978-1-78282-876-1 (hardcover)
ISBN: 978-1-78282-877-8 (softcover)

http://www.leonaur.com

Publisher's Notes

Contents

Opening Movements—The Mediterranean

Sir Julian S. Corbett

In the area of the Eastern Fleet the opening had been even more successful than in Home Waters and the Atlantic, but the operations in this theatre were so much entangled with combined expeditions that they can best be made clear at a later stage. It was only in the Mediterranean, where Admiral Souchon was in command of the *Goeben* and *Breslau*, that we had met with failure, and even there so little was its gravity recognised that generally it was regarded almost as a success. It will be recalled that the day after Admiral Milne had concentrated his force at Malta, he had been ordered to detach Admiral Troubridge's squadron, with the *Indefatigable, Indomitable, Gloucester* and eight destroyers, to shadow the *Goeben* and watch the entrance to the Adriatic.

The *Chatham* was to look into the Strait of Messina, and the *Dublin* had gone to Bizerta to get into touch with the French Admiral. About 1 a.m. on August 3, to give further precision to their orders, the Admiralty directed that the watch on the mouth of the Adriatic was to be maintained, but that the *Goeben* was the main objective, and she was to be shadowed wherever she went. Taking this as a repetition of the previous order which instructed him to remain near Malta himself, Admiral Milne stayed where he was and left the shadowing to Admiral Troubridge.

The whereabouts of the enemy was still uncertain. Circumstantial rumours told of their having arrived at Messina to coal, but by 8 a.m. the *Chatham* had run through the Strait and signalled they were not there. A report had also been received that there was a German collier at Majorca. Concluding, therefore, they must have gone west, and mindful that his primary object was to protect the French transport line, he ordered Admiral Troubridge to detach the *Gloucester* and his eight destroyers to watch the Adriatic, and with the rest of his force to proceed to the westward along the south coast of Sicily. In this way the admiral did his best to reconcile his instructions to watch the Adriatic, to shadow the enemy's cruisers, not to be brought to action by superior force and to cover the French transports.

An idea now arose at the Admiralty, owing perhaps to the unprotected state of our trade routes, that the *Goeben* and *Breslau* were making for the Atlantic. Early in the afternoon a patrol was ordered to be set up at Gibraltar, and Admiral Milne decided to take up a station in the Malta Channel. Accordingly, he gave orders for Admiral Troubridge to turn back for the entrance of the Adriatic with his own squadron, and for the two battle cruisers to carry on to a rendezvous twenty miles north-east of Valetta, where he would meet them. But at the Admiralty anxiety for the Atlantic trade routes had grown more insistent, and at 8.30 p.m. came an order for the two detached battle cruisers to proceed to the Strait of Gibraltar at high speed to prevent the *Goeben* leaving the Mediterranean. The Toulon Fleet had sailed at 4.0 that morning, and for over sixteen hours it had been making its way at twelve knots towards the Algerian coast, where it would bar any such attempt on the part of the Germans.

But we had not then sent our ultimatum, and organised connection between the British and French Admiralties had not yet been established. Consequently, the departure of the Toulon Fleet for the Algerian coast was not known to Admiral Milne till about noon on August 4, after the *Dublin* had reached Bizerta. Our Admiralty were informed sooner, but not till late on the night of the 3rd, through the Foreign Office. Nor was it till next evening that it was known from Paris that the transportation of the troops was not to begin at once, owing to the presence of the German ships. Consequently, they had to play up to the French hand as best they could, and Admiral Milne gave orders accordingly. Recalling the *Chatham*, who had reported nothing on the north coast of Sicily, he himself remained during the 3rd in the Malta Channel with the *Weymouth*, *Hussar* and three destroyers, while the two battle cruisers hurried off to the westward under Captain Kennedy of the *Indomitable*.

Though Admiral Souchon had gone west—having left the Straits ahead of the *Chatham*—it was not for Gibraltar he made. He was, in fact, making a dash at Bona and Philippeville to hamper the transport of the Eastern Division of the Nineteenth Army Corps. (*Stettiner*

ADMIRAL ARCHIBALD MILNE

Abendpost, June 6, 1915). Of what his ultimate destination was to be he as yet knew nothing; the probability was either Gibraltar or the Adriatic. Orders were hourly expected. About 6.0 p.m. he heard that war had been declared, and three hours later off the south coast of Sardinia the two ships separated, the *Goeben* making for Philippeville and the *Breslau* for Bona. At midnight his orders reached him. Their nature seems to have been entirely unexpected, for they directed the two ships to proceed to Constantinople. (Ludwig: *Die Fahrten der Goeben und der Breslau.*)

During the 3rd it would seem some kind of an arrangement had been made at Berlin on which it was assumed that he would be permitted to enter the Dardanelles. Long afterwards it became known that on the following day the Kaiser informed the Greek Minister that an alliance had been concluded between Germany and Turkey, and that the German warships in the Mediterranean were to join the Turkish Fleet and act in concert. (*Greek White Book,* 1917, No. 19.) This statement would appear to have been at least premature. Whatever may have been arranged with the Young Turk leaders, events went to show the Turkish Government was no party to it.

Though the new orders to Admiral Souchon were marked "of extreme urgency," he did not take them to cancel the enterprise in hand, and he carried on. At daybreak (August 4) both ports were subjected to a short bombardment. Some damage was done to the railway stations, and at Philippeville a magazine was blown up, but that was all. Nowhere were the troops embarking as had been intended. By the French Staff plan they should have been on their way in transports, sailing singly and unescorted under cover of the whole fleet operating to the eastward, but when on August 2 the *Goeben* was reported near Bizerta, Admiral de Lapeyrère stopped the movement and informed the Minister he must now proceed to form convoys. (Admiral Bienaimé in *La Libre Parole,* March 12, 1918.) After firing fifteen rounds Admiral Souchon left to rejoin the *Breslau.* His idea was first to proceed westward to give the impression that he intended to quit the Mediterranean. The two ships were then to meet at a rendezvous to the northward, and thence run back to the eastward. (Ludwig.)

Whether or not his intention was to make straight for the Dardanelles is unknown. It was possible; for a collier had been sent to Cape Matapan in the Morea to meet him. As a further precaution to escape observation, the course he took for the Levant lay between the two main trade routes. But here he was outwitted. For the result of the ef-

11

fort to evade was that he ran straight into the two British battle cruisers as they were hurrying westward. It was just after 10.30 a.m., some fifty miles westward of Galita Island, when the *Indomitable* sighted the two German cruisers coming eastward. The *Goeben* was seen at once to alter course to port, and Captain Kennedy altered to starboard in order to close, but the *Goeben* promptly turned away, and in a few minutes the two ships were passing each other on opposite courses at 8,000 yards. Guns were kept trained fore and aft, but neither side saluted, and after passing, Captain Kennedy led round in a wide circle and proceeded to shadow the *Goeben*, with his two ships on either quarter. The *Breslau* made off to the northward and disappeared, and early in the afternoon could be heard calling up the Cagliari wireless station.

By the time the Admiralty heard the *Goeben* had been found the decision was being taken to send an ultimatum to Germany. Two hours before it went out, they begged authority to order the battle cruisers to engage the *Goeben* if she attacked the French transports. That Bona had been bombarded was already known, and the authority was granted, subject to fair warning being given, but the message did not reach Admiral Milne till 5 p.m. At 2.5 p.m. word was sent him that the ultimatum had gone out, to expire at midnight, and he was told that this telegram cancelled the permission to attack the *Goeben*. This had not yet reached him, and it did not affect the situation.

Indeed, even before the permission came to hand, it was clear the *Goeben*, fresh from her overhaul, was getting away from our comparatively slow ships, which had not been in dock for some time and whose engine-rooms were understaffed. In her efforts to escape it is said she did two knots over her official speed, while the *Indomitable* could not reach her best. Captain Kennedy then ordered the *Indefatigable* and the *Dublin*, which had joined the chase from Bizerta, to carry on. Still the *Goeben* gained, and as the hours of our ultimatum were expiring only the *Dublin* had her in sight. Then she, too, lost the enemy, but found her again about 5 p.m., with the *Breslau* in company. She asked if she might engage the light cruiser, but the answer was "No!" and an order to continue shadowing.

Exasperating as it was to miss so good a chance just as the sands were running out, our ships were well disposed for trapping the enemy at Messina. It was Captain Kennedy's intention to hold off for the night so as not to give away his position to observers on the Sicilian coast. During the dark hours he meant to form a patrol in case the enemy should break back, and then close in so that at 4 a.m. he would

ADMIRAL ERNEST TROUBRIDGE

be off Messina. But this he was not permitted to do, for at the moment a political difficulty arose which could not be ignored and materially altered the strategical outlook. At 7 p.m. when Captain Kennedy was disposing his ships for closing the northern exit from the Straits, Admiral Milne received a message from the Admiralty to say that Italy had declared neutrality, and that in accordance with the terms of the declaration no ship was to go within six miles of her coast.

The declaration, therefore, seemed to bar Messina to both belligerents, and implicitly forbade any of his ships entering the Straits. It at least confirmed the impression that Admiral Souchon would go west, and on this supposition Admiral Milne made his dispositions for the night. The two detached battle cruisers, instead of carrying on to Messina, were to steer west at slow speed, the intention being that, as both of them wanted coaling, Bizerta should be used. The *Dublin* was to keep in touch, but she soon lost the chase, and about 10.0, being then off Cape San Vito, she turned to the westward and received an order to rejoin the *Indomitable* in the morning. The admiral took station off Valetta, with the *Chatham* and *Weymouth* watching on either side of Pantellaria. Admiral Troubridge was patrolling between Cephalonia and Cape Colonne in the heel of Italy, but with his cruiser squadron and the *Gloucester* only, for about midday, when Admiral Milne knew that war was imminent, he had ordered him to send the flotilla to Malta to coal.

Though the news of the ultimatum was sent off at 2 p.m., it did not reach Admiral Milne till 7.0. An hour and a half later he issued a new general order which was dominated by his original charge to cover the French transport line. The destroyers were turned back to the Greek coast and coal was to be sent to meet them, but there was considerable delay in getting the colliers away. Admiral Troubridge was to detach the *Gloucester* to watch the southern entrance of the Strait of Messina, and with his squadron to stand fast where he was, taking care not to get seriously engaged with a superior force. Then at 12.8 a.m. (5th) the flagship proceeded to the westward to join the other two battle cruisers and pick up the *Chatham* and *Weymouth* on the way. The admiral explained in his report:

> My first consideration was the protection of the French transports from the German ships. I knew they had at least three knots greater speed than our battle cruisers, and a position had to be taken up from which the *Goeben* could be cut off if she came westward.

Nevertheless, he had left the line of attack from Messina open, but, apart from this serious defect in his dispositions, they were in accordance with his original instructions. The order that the French transports were to be his first care had not been cancelled, though, in fact, there was now no need for him to concern himself with their safety.

When at 4 a.m. on August 3, a few hours after it was known that the *Goeben* had put into Messina, Admiral de Lapeyrère had put to sea with orders to seek out the enemy with his whole fleet and cover the transit of the troops in accordance with the Staff plan. To him, however, the situation had seemed too uncertain to adhere to it. Germany had not yet declared war, the attitude of Italy remained doubtful, and it was quite unknown whether Great Britain would come into the war or not. It was in these circumstances he had decided to abandon the Staff plan and to form convoys, and to this end he organised the fleet into three groups. In the first group, under Vice-Admiral Chocheprat, were the six "Lord Nelson" type battleships of the 1st Battle Squadron, *Diderot* (flag), *Danton, Vergniaud, Voltaire, Mirabeau,* and *Condorcet,* the 1st Division of the Armoured Cruiser Squadron, *Jules Michelet* (flag of Rear-Admiral de Sugny), *Ernest Renan* and *Edgar Quinet,* and a flotilla of twelve destroyers.

This group was to proceed to Philippeville. In the second group were the Dreadnought *Courbet,* carrying the commander-in-chief's flag, with the 2nd Battle Squadron *Patrie* (flag of Vice-Admiral Le Bris), *République, Démocratie, Justice* and *Vérité,* the 2nd Division of the Armoured Cruiser Squadron (*Léon Gambetta,* flag of Rear-Admiral Senès, *Victor Hugo, Jules Ferry*) and twelve more destroyers. This group was destined for Algiers. In the third group were the older ships of the Reserve Squadron, *Suffren, Gaulois, Bouvet,* and *Jauréguiberry,* under Rear-Admiral Guépratte, who was to go to Oran. The idea appears to have been that on reaching the latitude of the Balearic Islands the three groups would separate and each proceed to its assigned port. (Vedel: *Nos Marins à la Guerre.*)

This point was reached in the morning of August 4, when the fleet was about twenty-four hours out, and the news of the attack on Bona and Philippeville reached the Admiral and forced him to reconsider the plan. The situation was so far cleared that he knew Italy had declared her neutrality the previous evening, and so far as she was concerned it was possible for him to seek out the German cruisers and destroy them. But, on the other hand, the co-operation of the British Fleet was still uncertain, and an attempt to get contact with the enemy

ADMIRAL SOUCHON

might leave the transports exposed to attack. There was the further possibility, emphasised by the reported presence of a German collier in the Balearic Islands, that Admiral Souchon would seek to leave the Mediterranean and attack Algiers on his way to Gibraltar. Instead, therefore, of sending his first group to Philippeville, he ordered it to proceed with the second group at high speed to Cape Matifou, just to the eastward of Algiers, and there to take station on guard from 3 p.m. on the 4th till next day.

There was thus no occasion for Admiral Milne to trouble about the Western Mediterranean or the French transports, but he had received no word of Admiral de Lapeyrère's movements. Consequently, when at 1.15 a.m. on August 5 the order to commence hostilities against Germany reached him, and no modification of his general instructions accompanied it, he held to his disposition. After effecting his concentration to the west of Sicily he detached the *Indomitable* to Bizerta to coal and the *Dublin* to Malta, and with the *Inflexible, Indefatigable, Weymouth, Chatham,* and one division of destroyers proceeded to patrol between Sardinia and the African coast on the meridian 10° E., that is, to the northward of Bizerta.

At this time Sir Rennell Rodd, our ambassador at Rome, was trying to get a telegram through to say the enemy were in Messina, but, owing probably to the pressure on the wires, the message did not get to London till 6 p.m. Though the Germans were using Italian wireless freely, nothing came through from our Consul at Messina to the *Gloucester,* which was now watching the southern entrance of the Strait. At 3.35 p.m., however, Captain Howard Kelly telegraphed that the strength of wireless signals he was taking in indicated that the *Goeben* must be at Messina. She was, in fact, there coaling from a large East African liner, the *General,* which had been waiting for her. Admiral Milne, however, made no change in his dispositions; the last he had from the Admiralty was that, although Austria was not at war with France or England, he was to continue watching the Adriatic for the double purpose of preventing the Austrians emerging unobserved and preventing the Germans entering.

Admiral Troubridge was then cruising between Cape Colonne and Cephalonia with this object. He regarded the *Goeben,* owing to her speed and the range of her guns, (1912, Trial speed 27.2. Guns 10-11"; 12-5-9"), as in daylight a superior force to his own, with which his instructions were not to engage, but his intention was to neutralise the German advantage by engaging at night. Accordingly, in the afternoon of the 5th he steamed across towards Cape Colonne, but about 10 p.m., as Admiral Souchon had not come out, and as he knew there were Italian torpedo craft about, he turned back for his daylight position off Cephalonia. This he did with less hesitation, since, believing the French were guarding the approaches to the Western Mediterranean, he fully expected his two battle cruisers would now be returned to him.

Indeed, his impression was that when they were first attached to his flag it was a preliminary step to the whole command devolving on him. For in the provisional conversations with France it was understood that the British squadron at the outbreak of war would come automatically under the French commander-in-chief—an arrangement which necessarily involved the withdrawal of an officer of Admiral Milne's seniority. Admiral Milne, however, took an entirely different view, and feeling still bound by his "primary object," began at 7.30 a.m. on August 6 to sweep to the eastward, intending to be in the longitude of Cape San Vito, the north-west point of Sicily, by 6 p.m., "at which hour," so he afterwards explained, "the *Goeben* could have been sighted if she had left Messina," where he considered she was probably coaling.

The *Indomitable* at Bizerta was greatly delayed in coaling, so that it was not till 7 p.m. she was ready to sail, and then she received her orders—but they were not that she should reinforce Admiral Troubridge.

★★★★★★

The cause of the delay was that Captain Kennedy, finding the briquettes which were ready for him were no good, wished to coal from a British collier he found there with a suspiciously large cargo—over 5,000 tons—consigned on German account to Jiddah and Basra, and he required the commander-in-chief's authority to requisition it, though he began helping himself before the authority came.

★★★★★★

At 11 a.m., in response to an inquiry from the commander-in-chief, she had reported that the French transports had begun to move, and that Admiral de Lapeyrère, who had been last heard of at Algiers, was devoting his battle fleet—not on the British plan to cover the line of passage—but entirely to escort duty, and that it would not be free till the 10th. The French admiral was, in fact, no longer at Algiers. For on the 5th, finding the Germans did not appear, he had broken up the

20

COMMANDING OFFICER OF THE *GOEBEN*,
RICHARD ACKERMANN

Cape Matifou guard and proceeded himself, with the flagship and two ships of the 2nd Battle Squadron, to search the Balearic Islands, leaving the rest of the squadron to carry on with the escort programme, (Vedel), and apparently detaching a squadron of four armoured and three or four light cruisers to Philippeville. For, with the other information, Admiral Milne heard from the *Indomitable* at Bizerta that this squadron had left Philippeville that morning at 8.0 for Ajaccio in Corsica. The messages, however, were not very clear and seem to have left Admiral Milne unchanged in his conviction that his duty was to close the northern exit of the Straits of Messina. The *Indomitable* was therefore ordered to join him thirty-five miles west of Milazzo, so that with his full force he could proceed to bar the Germans' escape for the night. If they eluded him, he intended to chase to the northward for the Strait of Bonifacio, or Cape Corso in the north of Corsica.

The reason for these dispositions was clearly a belief that the Germans might still have an intention to attack the French convoys, and so long as this was a practical possibility the Admiral could scarcely disregard his strict injunctions to protect them. We know now that Admiral Souchon had no such reckless intention. From all accounts he believed himself caught. At Messina he had hoped to coal, but facilities of wharfage were denied him, and he had to do what he could from German colliers he found there. His belief was that the French cruisers were watching to the northward, and that the main part of the British Fleet was about the Strait of Otranto, with its scouts off the Strait of Messina. The urgent order from Berlin that he was to endeavour to make the Dardanelles had not been cancelled, and the venture seemed more like a forlorn hope than ever; all the officers, it is said, made their wills.

So desperate indeed was the chance that in spite of the ominous outlook in the Near East it was the only one which had not entered into our calculations. Our relations with Turkey were severely strained, owing to our having, the day before war was declared, requisitioned the two Dreadnoughts which were just being completed for her in British yards. We knew she was mobilising and that the German Military Mission was taking charge of her army, but we also knew the Dardanelles was being mined. Nothing of all this vital information was communicated to Admiral Milne, except the fact of the minelaying, and if this detail had any effect upon his judgment it would tend to show that Constantinople was barred to all belligerents alike. That Germany, with the load she already had upon her, intended to attempt the absorption of Turkey was then beyond belief.

All this was in the dark when Admiral Milne, feeling bound by his instructions that "the *Goeben* was his objective," made his last dispositions to prevent her escape to the northward. But scarcely had he issued his instructions when Captain Kelly in the *Gloucester*, being then off Taormina, signalled the enemy coming south. Admiral Souchon's intention, as his one chance of escape, was to steer a false course till nightfall, so as to give the impression he was making back to join the Austrians in the Adriatic, and as his reserve ammunition had been sent to Pola, this was probably the original plan before the intervention of Great Britain rendered that sea nothing but a trap.

The orders he issued were that the *Goeben* would leave at 5 p.m. at seventeen knots; the *Breslau* would follow five miles astern, closing up at dark; while the *General*, sailing two hours later, would keep along the Sicilian coast and make, by a southerly track, for Santorin, the most southerly island of the Archipelago, (Ludwig.) The two cruisers, after steering their false course till dark, would make for Cape Matapan, where, as we have seen, a collier had been ordered to meet them. In accordance with this plan, Admiral Souchon, the moment he sighted the *Gloucester*, altered course to port so as to keep along the coast of Calabria outside the six-mile limit.

When at 6.10 p.m. Admiral Milne got the news, he was thirty-five miles north of Marittimo, proceeding eastward to his new rendezvous north of Sicily, but as the passage of the Strait was denied him, he at once turned back. His idea was that Admiral Troubridge, with his squadron and his eight destroyers, besides two more which were being hurried off to him from Malta in charge of the *Dublin*, was strong enough to bar the Adriatic, and that there was still a possibility of the Germans making back to the westward along the south of Sicily. The Admiralty, however, an hour and a half later sent him an order to chase through the Strait if the enemy went south. Unfortunately, it did not come to hand till midnight, too late for the Admiral to modify the movement to which he was committed.

All this time Captain Kelly was clinging to the two German ships and reporting their course. It was not done without difficulty. At 7.30, being on their seaward beam, he began to lose sight of them against the land in the gathering darkness, and he saw his only chance was to get the inshore position and have the moon right when it rose. But to effect his purpose he must steer straight for the *Goeben*, well knowing if she opened fire he would be blown out of the water. Yet he did

SMS *Breslau*

not hesitate, and by his daring move succeeded in gaining the desired position well upon the enemy's port quarter. This position he held till the *Breslau* altered towards the land and forced him, after a struggle, to fall astern for lack of sea room. Then she turned to cross his bows, as though she meant fighting. Captain Kelly altered to meet her and they passed starboard to starboard at about 4,000 yards. Still feeling it his duty to follow the *Goeben*, he did not open fire, and the *Breslau* disappeared east-south-eastwards, presumably to ascertain if the main British force was in that direction. So, the shadowing went on till about 10.45, south of Cape Rizzuto, the *Goeben* suddenly turned to about S. 60° E., and began trying to jam the *Gloucester*'s signals.

By this time the *Breslau* had probably reported all clear in that direction. Admiral Troubridge was, in fact, off the Greek coast. When the *Goeben* came out of the Strait he was patrolling with his four cruisers (*Defence*-flag, *Warrior, Duke of Edinburgh, Black Prince*) off Cephalonia on the lookout for a German collier. His destroyers, with scarcely any coal in their bunkers, were all either at Santa Maura or patrolling outside. (Their collier had been ordered to Port Vathi in Ithaca, but the Greek skipper had gone to another port of the same name.) His intention, as we have seen, had been to seek an engagement only at dusk, but Admiral Milne had ordered him to leave a night action to his destroyers. On hearing the enemy were out, he at once steamed north-north-east towards Santa Maura, thinking they might be making for his base behind the island, and, with the same idea, he ordered his eight destroyers to be under way and hidden in Vasilico Bay by midnight.

As soon, however, as he knew the *Goeben* was heading for the Adriatic, he held on for the position he originally intended to take at Fano Island, just north of Corfu, where he hoped the confined and shoal waters would enable him to force an action at his own range. Even when Captain Kelly reported the *Goeben*'s change of course he believed it was only a device to throw him off, and it was not till midnight, when the *Gloucester*, in spite of the *Goeben*'s efforts to jam, reported her still going south-east, that he was convinced her original course was the false one and that she was making for the Eastern Mediterranean, either to operate against our trade or to repeat at Port Said and Alexandria what she had done at the Algerian ports. He then turned to the south to intercept her, called out his destroyers, and signalled to Captain John Kelly, who in the *Dublin* was bringing up the two destroyers from Malta, to head off the chase.

★★★★★★

Captain John Kelly when he heard the *Goeben* was heading for the Adriatic, calculating he could overtake her with his two destroyers next morning, had asked leave to deliver a daylight attack, but permission was refused and he was told to follow the rear-admiral's orders.

✶✶✶✶✶✶

The *Dublin* had already received orders to the same effect from Admiral Milne, who, as soon as it became clear that the enemy was making to the eastward, ran for Malta to coal so as to be able to keep to the chase.

Guided by his brother's signals, Captain John Kelly and his two destroyers made for the zone in which it seemed the two German ships were intending to get together again, and about 1 a.m. he saw smoke. It was now brilliant moonlight, so that the work in hand was extremely hazardous. Still, as soon as he had gained a good position for delivering an attack he carried on to close the chase, till in a few minutes he became aware from the *Gloucester's* signals that the ship he was after must be not the *Goeben* but the *Breslau*, and that the *Goeben* must be between him and his brother.

He therefore turned to meet her, and after getting across her course so as to have the moon right, he ran up to attack from ahead. It was a most promising situation. But he was doomed to disappointment. The *Goeben* was nowhere to be seen. Possibly warned by her consort, she had altered course to avoid the torpedo menace, but the failure may have been due to some confusion between local and Greenwich time in taking in the *Gloucester's* signals. Whatever the cause, she had given the *Dublin* the slip, and there was nothing to do but to carry on to the Fano rendezvous according to previous instructions.

At the same time (3.50 a.m.) Admiral Troubridge, being then abreast of Zante, also gave up the chase. He had received no authority to quit his position, nor any order to support the *Gloucester*. His intention had been to engage the *Goeben* if he could get contact before 6 a.m., since that was the only chance of his being able to engage her closely enough for any prospect of success, and when he found it impossible he thought it his duty not to risk his squadron against an enemy who, by his superiority in speed and gun-power, could choose his distance and outrange him. Still, he only slowed down, and held on as he was, in expectation that his two battle cruisers would now be sent back to him, with instructions for concerting action. But they did not come, and about 10 a.m. on August 7, by which time the *Goeben*

H.M.S. BLACK PRINCE. Armoured Cruiser, 13,550 tons.

Cost £1,150,000; Length, 480 feet; Beam, 73½ feet; Draught, 27½ feet; Speed, 22½ knots. Armed with Six 9.2 in.; Ten 6 in.; Twenty Small Quick Firing Guns, and Three Torpedo Tubes.

had passed ahead of him, he went into Zante preparatory to resuming his watch in the Adriatic.

When Admiral Troubridge made the port, the commander-in-chief steaming at moderate speed was nearing Malta. During the night he had received from the French Admiral an offer of a squadron which he had requested should patrol between Marsala and Cape Bon to watch the passage between Sicily and Africa. (The ships were the armoured cruisers *Bruix, Latouche-Tréville, Amiral Charner* and the cruiser *Jurien de la Gravière.*) Being thus relieved of anxiety in that direction he had moved away to the eastward at fifteen knots. The *Indomitable* was coming up astern at twenty-one knots, and when she reached Malta, he did not send her on, but kept her there till his other two ships had coaled. Thus, Captain Kelly in the *Gloucester* was left to carry on the chase alone. So perilous was his position that, about 5.30 a.m., Admiral Milne had signalled to him to drop astern so as to avoid capture; but he chose to take the signal as permissive only, and held on as doggedly as ever in spite of every effort of the Germans to shake him off. By 10.30 a.m. the *Breslau* had rejoined, and, after taking station astern of the flagship, kept crossing the *Gloucester's* course as though to drop mines.

But Captain Kelly did not flinch. He steamed on undisturbed and with so much persistence that off the Gulf of Kalamata the *Breslau* began to try to ride him off by dropping astern. By 1 p.m. it became clear that something must be done if he was to keep the *Goeben* in sight. By engaging the *Breslau,* he would be able either to force her to close the flagship or bring the flagship back to protect her. At 1.35, therefore, he opened fire with his forward six-inch gun at 11,500 yards. The *Breslau,* who was two points on his port bow and had her starboard guns bearing, returned the fire smartly and accurately. Captain Kelly then increased to full speed, ran up to 10,000, and, turning 10 points to port, brought the enemy on his starboard quarter. As soon as the two ships were engaged broadside to broadside, the *Goeben,* as Captain Kelly expected, turned 16 points to come back, and, though far out of range, she opened fire.

Having thus gained his object, Captain Kelly at 1.50 ceased fire and, with admirable judgment, broke off the action, considering it his duty to preserve his ship intact for fulfilling his main duty of keeping hold of the *Goeben,* and as soon as she turned again to resume her eastward course he informed the commander-in-chief and continued to shadow. Admiral Milne, who was coaling, had not yet felt able to

31

leave Malta, and was getting very anxious for the *Gloucester*. Knowing she must be short of coal, he sent her orders not to chase further than Cape Matapan, and then to rejoin Admiral Troubridge, but no other cruiser was sent to take her place. By 4.40 p.m. the *Gloucester* had reached the specified point, the *Goeben* and *Breslau* could be seen holding eastwards through the Cervi Channel, and with this last report of their movements Captain Kelly turned back.

For his conduct throughout the affair he was highly commended by the Admiralty. The minute on his report ran:

> The *Goeben* could have caught and sunk the *Gloucester* at any time . . . she was apparently deterred by the latter's boldness, which gave the impression of support close at hand. The combination of audacity with restraint, unswerving attention to the principal military object, *viz.* holding on to the *Goeben* and strict conformity to orders, constitute a naval episode which may justly be regarded as a model.

In endorsement of this judgment Captain Kelly received the honour of Companionship of the Bath.

His conduct was the one bright spot in the unfortunate episode. The outcome of a situation which had been so promising, and which might well have resulted in a success, priceless at the opening of the war, was a severe disappointment. But on his return home the commander-in-chief was able to give explanations of his difficulties which satisfied the Board and he was exonerated from blame. In view of the instructions which the Admiralty had given him in their anxiety to protect the French transport line and to respect the neutrality of Italy, it is clear that what blame there was could not rest solely on the shoulders of the Admiral. His failure was due at least in part to the fact that owing to the rapid changes in the situation, it was practically impossible for the Admiralty to keep him adequately informed. The sudden pressure on an embryonic staff organisation was more than it could bear, but the fact remains that intelligence essential for forming a correct appreciation of the shifting situation either did not reach him, or reached him too late, and, what was more embarrassing, his original instructions as to his "primary object" were not cancelled when they were rendered obsolete by the action of the Toulon Fleet.

After due consideration it was felt that the failure of Admiral Troubridge to bring the *Goeben* to action required investigation. A month later, therefore, he was recalled to justify himself before a Court of

Battle Cruiser SMS Goeben

Inquiry. On its report, a Court Martial was ordered, before which he was charged under the Third Section of the Naval Discipline Act, that:

> From negligence or default he did on August 7 forbear to pursue the chase of H.I.G.M.'s ship *Goeben*, being an enemy then flying.

But before a full Court of his brother officers Admiral Troubridge had no difficulty in proving his case. The Court found that he had acted in accordance with his instructions, that he was justified in regarding the enemy's force as superior to his own in daylight, and that, although if he had carried on the chase he might have brought the *Goeben* to action in the Cervi Channel, he would not have been justified in quitting the station assigned to him without further orders. Consequently they declared the charge not proved, and the admiral was "fully and honourably" acquitted. There the matter ended.

Much as there was in these crowded opening days to excuse the failure, it must always tell as a shadow in our naval history. But it is only right to recall that the circumstances of the case are closely analogous to those in which Nelson in 1805, preoccupied primarily with the security of Sicily and the Eastern Mediterranean, allowed Villeneuve to escape to the west, as Admiral Souchon had been permitted to escape to the east. Nor is this the only precedent; for it was in these same hide-and-seek waters that Nelson's great successor Collingwood had missed Ganteaume and Allemande in 1809. Tried beside the failure of the two great masters in whom all our old naval lore culminated, it will perhaps be judged most leniently by those whose wisdom and knowledge are the ripest.

What makes the whole episode more unfortunate is that, had we been able to know it in time to take action, there was still a possibility of making good the failure of the first blow. Whatever may have been the truth about the alleged alliance between Germany and Turkey, it was clearly not working. For scarcely had Admiral Souchon shaken off the *Gloucester* and entered the Aegean Sea when a message reached him that he must not proceed at once to the Dardanelles, as the Turks were making difficulties about allowing him to enter. He was still, therefore, in a highly precarious position, and immediately took steps to get contact with the *Loreley*, the German guardship at Constantinople. To this end, at the risk of revealing his position, he signalled to the *General* to make forthwith for Smyrna instead of Santorini in order to act as wireless link.

His other collier he had picked up at the pre-arranged rendezvous, and, having found a convenient bay to hide her, proceeded to cruise slowly eastward amongst the islands. During the 8th, while thus engaged, he fell in with two French passenger ships with a large number of reservists from the Bosporus, but as they kept within Greek waters, he had to leave them alone. In the afternoon, getting no further instructions, he sent away the *Breslau* to fetch his collier and bring her into Denusa, a small and sparsely inhabited island east of Naxos, and there they coaled during the night.

Meanwhile Admiral Milne had taken up the chase again, but it was not till midnight (the 7th-8th) that he left Malta, and as in default of intelligence he steamed very slowly, at 2.30 p.m. on the 8th he was no more than half way to Matapan. Then fortune played another trick, for here he received from the Admiralty a warning, which had been sent out by mistake, that hostilities had commenced against Austria. He could not yet tell whether the *Goeben's* objective might not be Alexandria and our Levant and Eastern trade, but since his last news of the French Fleet was that it would not be free to co-operate with him before the 10th, his only course seemed to be to turn back and re-concentrate his fleet. He therefore proceeded to a position 100 miles south-westward of Cephalonia so as to prevent the Austrians cutting him off from his base, and ordered Admiral Troubridge to join him.

The *Gloucester* and the destroyers were to do the same, while the *Dublin* and *Weymouth* were left to watch the Adriatic. Later on in the day, (August 8), he was informed that the alarm was false, but as, at the same time, he was instructed that relations with Austria were critical, he continued his movement for concentration till noon on the 9th. Then came a telegram from the Admiralty to say definitely we were not at war with Austria and that he was to resume the chase. Accordingly, leaving Admiral Troubridge to watch the Adriatic, he proceeded south-eastwards with the three battle cruisers and the *Weymouth*, calling the *Dublin* and *Chatham* to follow. The movement involved some risk, since, for the time, it left Admiral Troubridge in the air, but as the Admiralty were inviting the French to use Malta as their base it could not be long before they would arrive to join him.

Since Admiral Milne came down the Greek coast at only ten knots, presumably to allow his light cruisers to come up, it was not till 3 a.m. on August 10 that he entered the Aegean, some sixty hours after the *Goeben* had passed the Cervi Channel, and he was still entirely without information as to her whereabouts or object. Admiral Souchon was actually still at Denusa, waiting to hear that permission to enter the Dardanelles had been negotiated. But not a word could the *General* pass him of any alteration in the situation. The previous evening (9th) she had been ordered to make for the Dardanelles. Hour after hour went by in increasing anxiety, till about 9 p.m. he had begun to hear the wireless of the British. As it came nearer and nearer his position became too dangerous to hold, and although he was still without a word from Constantinople, he decided to make for the Dardanelles at all costs, determined, so his officers believed, to force an entrance if it were denied him. He had finished coaling at 5 a.m. on the 10th, and three-quarters of an hour later he put to sea.

At this time Admiral Milne having rounded Cape Malea, was heading about north-east on a course that was rapidly converging with that of Admiral Souchon. He was well in sight of Belo Pulo Light, and little more than 100 miles to the westward of the German cruisers. But close as he now was upon their track it was too late. Even had he known what their destination was he could scarcely have been up in time to prevent them being piloted safely through the Dardanelles minefields. Nor had he any good reason for making the effort. So far as he was informed of the state of affairs, the immediate danger was for the safety of Alexandria and the Suez Canal. Apart from this there was still a widespread opinion that Admiral Souchon's intention was to rejoin the Austrians. He had had plenty of time to coal amongst the islands; indeed, there was a report that he had gone to Syra for that purpose.

Admiral Milne's main preoccupation, therefore, was to make sure the enemy did not break back to the southward, and with this object in view he spread his force so as to bar the passages through the islands between the mainland and the Cyclades, while the *Weymouth* was detached to look into Milo and Syra. Soon, however, German signals were heard nearby, and a sweep was made to the southward. Then the German colliers were heard calling distinctly to the northward, and so the sweep turned in that direction to occupy the passage between Nikaria and Mykoni, while the *Weymouth* scouted as high as Smyrna, and *Chatham*, who after searching round Naxos had just joined, was sent to the eastward to examine the vicinity of Kos. But all doubt was soon to be at an end. Shortly before noon on the 11th, before the sweep was complete, the admiral heard from Malta that the *Goeben* and *Breslau* had entered the Dardanelles at 8.30 the previous night. They had, in fact, anchored off Cape Helles about 5.0 that evening, still not knowing whether they would be received. But on calling for a pilot, a steamboat came out and signalled them to follow. As soon as the news reached Admiral Milne he hurried off after them, and in the course of the afternoon received an order to blockade the exit.

So, the unhappy affair ended in something like a burst of public derision that the Germans should so soon have been chased out of the Mediterranean to suffer an ignominious internment. How false was that consolation none but the best informed could then even dream? It was many months before it was possible to appreciate fully the combined effrontery, promptitude and sagacity of the move. When we consider that the Dardanelles was mined, that no permission to enter it had been ratified, and that everything depended on the German powers of cajolery at Constantinople, when we also recall the world-wide results that ensued, it is not too much to say that few naval decisions more bold and well-judged were ever taken. So completely, indeed, did the risky venture turn a desperate situation into one of high moral and material advantage, that for the credit of German statesmanship it goes far to balance the cardinal blunder of attacking France through Belgium.

★★★★★★

It would appear that the final decision was taken by Admiral Souchon himself. According to Admiral von Tirpitz, when on August 3 news was received of the alleged alliance with Turkey, orders were sent to Admiral Souchon to attempt to break through to the Dardanelles. On August 5 the German Embassy at Constantinople reported that in view of the situation there it was undesirable for the ships to arrive for the present. Thereupon the orders for the Dardanelles were cancelled, and Admiral Souchon, who was then coaling at Messina, was directed to proceed to Pola or else break out into the Atlantic. Later in the day, however, Austria, in spite of the pressure that was being put upon her from Berlin to declare war, protested she was not yet in a position to help with her fleet. In these circumstances it was thought best to give Admiral Souchon liberty to decide for himself which line of escape to attempt, and he then chose the line of his first instructions. (Von Tirpitz, *My Memories*.)

★★★★★★

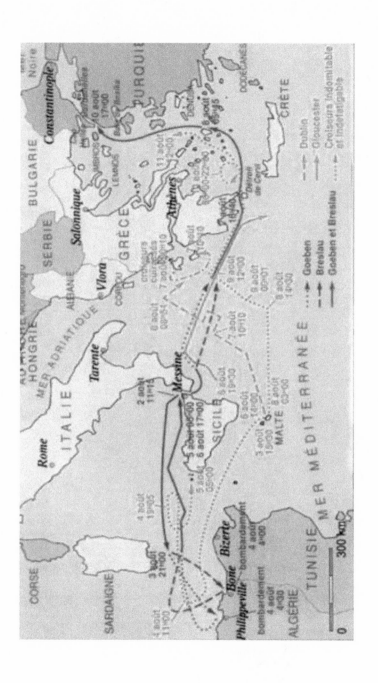

The Flight of the "Goeben" and "Breslau"

Preface

After the publication in March, 1920, of the *Official History of the War: Naval Operations, Vol. I.* by Sir Julian S. Corbett, I represented to the First Lord of the Admiralty that the book contained serious inaccuracies, and made a formal request that the Admiralty should take action in the matter. As the Admiralty did not think proper to accede to my request, I have thought it right to publish the following narrative.

A. Berkeley Milne.
Admiral.

January 1921.

CHAPTER 1

Official Responsibility

In justice to the public, to the officers and men who served under my command, and to my own reputation, I have thought it right to publish the following narrative of the events in the Mediterranean immediately preceding and following upon the outbreak of war, concerning which there has been, and is, some unfortunate misapprehension.

During the war, when secrecy with regard to naval operations was necessary, it was natural that the public anxiety should find expression in conjectures, and that false impressions should prevail. I select the following passages from Hansard as examples:—

Hansard (House of Commons), 31st July, 1916. Escape of the *Goeben* and *Breslau* (Despatches).

Commander Bellairs asked the First Lord of the Admiralty, in view of the fact that the disasters of the Dardanelles and the Baghdad advance are about to be inquired into by Commissions, whether he is aware that the entry of Turkey into the war originated in the escape of the *Goeben* and *Breslau* from Messina to the Dardanelles in August 1914; and whether he can now publish the despatches dealing with the matter, together with the dispositions of ships of which the Board of Admiralty have expressed their approval?

Dr. Macnamara: The Admiralty have hitherto only published despatches which deal with actual engagements, and not reports on the disposal of His Majesty's ships, whether or not those dispositions succeeded in bringing about an engagement. My right hon. friend (the First Lord, Mr. Balfour), does not propose to depart from this well-established practice. He must not be assumed as giving unqualified concurrence to the view of my

45

hon. and gallant friend that the entry of Turkey into the war originated with the arrival of these two ships at Constantinople.

12th March, 1919.

Mr. H. Smith asked the First Lord of the Admiralty whether he will lay upon the Table of the House the Report of the proceedings of the Court of Inquiry which inquired into the circumstances attending the escape of the *Goeben* and *Breslau*, and which acquitted Admiral Sir Berkeley Milne of all responsibility therefor?

Dr. Macnamara: As stated in reply to a question by my hon. friend the Member for Portsmouth North, on the 26th February, no Court of Inquiry was held in the case of Admiral Sir Berkeley Milne. The Admiralty issued a statement on the 30th August, 1914, to the effect that:—

> The conduct and dispositions of Admiral Sir Berkeley Milne in regard to the German vessels *Goeben* and *Breslau* have been the subject of the careful examination of the Board of Admiralty, with the result that their Lordships have approved the measures taken by him in all respects.

These, and other perfectly correct statements of the Government on the subject, did not, however, serve to dispel the misapprehensions to which I refer.

The Government have consistently refused to publish the documents concerning the opening of the war in the Mediterranean, the reason for their refusal being that the history of the affair would be related in the *Official History* of the war, in preparation by Sir Julian Corbett. On the 15th November, 1920, for instance, the Parliamentary Secretary to the Admiralty stated in the House of Commons that:—

> So far as the near future is concerned, it is not proposed to publish the documents in regard to the escape of the *Goeben* . . the matter had already been . . . dealt with in the *Naval History of the War*.

It was, therefore, to be expected that the facts of the episode in question would be impartially set forth in the *Official History of the War: Naval Operations*, by Sir Julian S. Corbett, Vol. 1, published in March 1920.

That expectation has not been fulfilled. Nor have the Admiralty thought proper to take any action to correct the erroneous impression which, in my own view, is disengaged by the official historian's presentation of the case. Indeed, a reference to the statement of Sir James Craig, quoted above, shows that the Admiralty profess to regard the account of the matter written by Sir Julian Corbett as an exact version of the documents upon which the historian's version of them was founded. It is not a conclusion I find myself able to accept.

If, writing as an independent historian, Sir Julian Corbett was impelled to criticise the conduct of the naval operations by the officers in command of them, I should hold that the admirals at sea, being professional seamen, were probably better able to judge of the requirements of the situation than an amateur on shore, and the matter would resolve itself into a simple difference of opinion. But the case is not so simple as that. Neither the Committee of Imperial Defence nor the Admiralty can be absolved from a definite share in the responsibility for the *Official History*.

The First Lord of the Admiralty stated on 18th February, 1920, that the *Official History* is being compiled *under the direction of the Committee of Imperial Defence* (Hansard, 18th February, 1920). The same statement was made by the Parliamentary Secretary to the Admiralty on 27th October, 1920 (Hansard).

The prime minister informed the House of Commons on 1st November, 1920, that:—

> Sir Julian Corbett, I understand, is writing the official account of the war from the Admiralty point of view (Hansard, 1st November, 1920).

On the cover of the *Official History* appear the words "Official History of the War." Inside, facing the title-page, appears a note, as follows:

> The Lords Commissioners of the Admiralty have given the Author access to official documents in the preparation of the work, but they are in no way responsible for his reading or presentation of the facts as stated.

The contradiction is obvious.

Sir Julian Corbett's own account of his position is explained by him in the following letter, published in *The Nineteenth Century and After,* November 1920, referring to an article by Admiral Eardley Wilmot appearing in the previous issue:—

WHO LET THE *GOEBEN* ESCAPE?
To the Editor of *The Nineteenth Century*.

Sir,

In an able and dispassionate appreciation of the escape of the *Goeben* appearing in your issue of this month, your contributor gives the weight of his name to a widely prevailing impression which I would beg leave to correct.

Referring to the *Official Naval History of the War*, as the main source for the facts of the case, he says, 'As regards this incident, it has evidently been heavily censored.' That such an impression is natural, I do not deny, but it is entirely untrue. I was given the freest possible access to the secret files which contain the telegrams that passed between the Admiralty and the admiral, as well as to the instructions, logs and the rest, and from these sources a narrative was constructed to the best of my ability. *After being tested for accuracy of detail by senior officers who were engaged in the operations*, it was submitted to the Admiralty, and, after careful examination, returned to me, *with a few suggestions as to the wording of certain passages*. Beyond this, no 'censoring' took place, and *the tenor of the comments remained unchanged*.

The narrative was not censored at all, nor was any telegram relating to operations ignored or misrepresented in the text.

In regard to this episode—and indeed to the whole volume—I can only look upon the Admiralty 'censoring,' such as it was, *as frank assistance in securing an accurate, full and impartial record of what occurred,*

Yours obediently,

(Sgd.) Julian S. Corbett.

My italics—A. B. M.

It will be observed that Sir Julian Corbett, while denying that the Admiralty "censored" his account of the matter, definitely states that it was submitted to the Admiralty, and that their Lordships made "a few suggestions as to the wording of certain passages." He adds that "the tenor of the comments remained unchanged."

It is, therefore, clear, first, that the Admiralty reserve to themselves the right to suggest alterations in the text; second, that, in the case under consideration, their Lordships made no such alterations in "the tenor of the comments." It is the "tenor of the comments" to which I take grave exception. Sir Julian writes:—

I can only look upon the Admiralty 'censoring,' such as it was, as frank assistance in securing an accurate, full and impartial record of what occurred.

It is a view with which I regret I cannot agree. Sir Julian Corbett further states that his narrative was "tested for accuracy of detail by senior officers who were engaged in the operations." That is a statement I am quite unable to understand. I was commander-in-chief in the Mediterranean at the period in question; I came home in August 1914; and neither then nor subsequently did Sir Julian Corbett communicate with me. I did not see his account of the episode until the *Official History* was published in March 1920. I regard it as extremely unfortunate (at least) that Sir Julian Corbett should permit himself to assert, or to imply, that his narrative was submitted to me before publication. After the publication of the book, I called upon Sir Julian, and, expressing my regret that he had not consulted me, when I should have had great pleasure in giving him all the assistance in my power to obtain accurate information, I asked him why he had not availed himself of my services. Sir Julian was, however, unable to afford me any explanation of his failure to do so.

According to the statements of ministers, Sir Julian Corbett is compiling his history "under the directions of the Committee of Imperial Defence," and "from the Admiralty point of view." Whether or not it is possible logically to reconcile Sir Julian's own account of his position, with the official definitions of it, the public will, I think, agree that it is the duty of the Committee of Imperial Defence, and of the Board of Admiralty, who are jointly responsible for the *Official History*, to protect from aspersion the reputation of His Majesty's officers.

The prime minister stated on 1st November that:—

The preparation of the history is a charge on the Treasury Vote for the Committee of Imperial Defence, to whom Sir Julian Corbett is responsible as author (Hansard, 1st November, 1920).

The cost of the *Official History*, therefore, is defrayed out of public money; and the public have the right to demand that the Committee of Imperial Defence should ensure accuracy and impartiality in official publications for which the Committee are responsible.

In the case under consideration, there is presented the curious anomaly of a narrative, the proofs of which were passed, "with a few suggestions," by the Admiralty but of which the "tenor of the comments" contradicts the statement of the Admiralty, published by the

Board on 30th August, 1914, and read to the House of Commons by the Parliamentary Secretary to the Admiralty on 12th March, 1919, that:—

The conduct and dispositions of Admiral Sir Berkeley Milne in regard to the German vessels *Goeben* and *Breslau* have been the subject of the careful examination of the Board of Admiralty, with the result that their Lordships have approved the measures taken by him in all respects.

In what that conduct and those dispositions and measures consisted, it is my purpose to relate in the following pages.

CHAPTER 2

The Situation in July 1914

At the end of July 1914, the force under my command in the Mediterranean consisted of the three battle cruisers of the Second Battle Cruiser Squadron, the four armoured cruisers of the First Cruiser Squadron, commanded by Rear-Admiral C. T. Troubridge, four light cruisers and fourteen destroyers.

******

Mediterranean Fleet

Commander-in-Chief: Admiral Sir A. Berkeley Milne, Bt., G.C.V.O., K.C.B.; Chief of Staff: Commodore Richard F. Phillimore, C.B., M.V.O.

Second Battle Cruiser Squadron

Inflexible (8-12"), flag of C.-in-C.
Captain Arthur N. Loxley.
Indefatigable (8-12").
Captain Charles F. Sowerby.
Indomitable (8-12").
Captain Francis W. Kennedy.

First Cruiser Squadron

Rear-Admiral C. T. Troubridge, C.B., C.M.G., M.V.O.
Defence (4-9-2", 10-7-5"), flag of R.-A.
Captain Fawcet Wray.
Black Prince (6-9-2", 10-6").
Captain Frederick D. Gilpin-Brown.
Duke of Edinburgh (6-9-2", 10-6").
Captain Henry Blackett.
Warrior (6-9-2", 4-7-5").
Captain George H. Borrett,

Chatham (8-6").

Captain Sidney R. Drury-Lowe.

Dublin (8-6").

Captain John D. Kelly.

Gloucester (2-6", 10-4").

Captain W. A. Howard Kelly, M.V.O.

Weymouth (8-6").

Captain William D. Church.

★★★★★★

In order that the situation in the Mediterranean may be understood, it is necessary to indicate the relative strength in effective heavy ships of the other naval Powers in July 1914. France, shortly to become our Ally, possessed one Dreadnought, six "Dantons" and five other battleships. Austria-Hungary, a member of the Triple Alliance, possessed three Dreadnoughts and three other battleships. Italy, also a member at that time of the Triple Alliance, possessed three Dreadnoughts, and four other battleships. Germany had placed the *Goeben*, battle cruiser, and the *Breslau*, light cruiser, in the Mediterranean. In respect of heavy ships, therefore, the position was:—

France	12	Germany	1
Great Britain	8	Austria	6
		Italy	7
	—		—
	15		14

But a numerical comparison affords only a partial indication of the real position. Opposing navies are very seldom all in one place at one time. A squadron of one fleet may be attacked by the full strength of another fleet. France, if required to deal with Austria, might have been outnumbered by the accession of Italy. The three battle cruisers of Great Britain were liable to be hopelessly overwhelmed by either Austria or Italy.

At the end of July 1914, when war was expected, the possibility that both Austria and Italy would join Germany must be considered, and the instructions which I received from the Admiralty were framed in accordance with that contingency. Whether or not the possibility was considered that the Ottoman Empire would side with Germany, was not known to me. In June, I had visited Constantinople in *Inflexible*. At that date, mines had already been laid in the Straits of the Dardanelles; and, in following the channel, we were brought within close range of the shore batteries.

In Constantinople, I was received with the greatest courtesy by the authorities, who did their utmost to make my visit pleasant. H.M. the *Sultan* honoured me, together with the officers of my staff, with an invitation to dine at Yildiz Kiosk, upon which occasion the *grand vizier* and all the ministers were present, except Enver Pasha, who was absent from Constantinople. I went to see the Royal stables, and visited an Anatolëan Cavalry Regiment. H.R.H. the Crown Prince came on board the flagship, H.M.S. *Inflexible*, His Royal Highness had not visited the *Goeben*, when, a few months before. Admiral Souchon's flagship was at Constantinople. I mention these incidents of our reception, because (among others) they gave no suggestion of anti-English sympathies on the part of Turkish officials, but rather indicated most friendly feelings towards Great Britain.

I was asked to inspect the Turkish crew which was on the point of leaving to take over the battleship built in England for Turkey. They arrived in England, but their ship, together with another vessel also built for Turkey, was acquired by Great Britain. These deprivations probably exercised a considerable effect on Turkish opinion; for the ships had been built by subscription, and their arrival was eagerly expected by the Turkish Ministers, and especially by Djemal Pasha, Minister of Marine, who had intended to go to England and to return in one of the new vessels.

CHAPTER 3

Preliminary Dispositions

Such was the general situation in the Mediterranean when, on
27th July, 1914, I received from the Admiralty the preliminary telegram of warning. On that day, the greater part of the British Fleet
was at Alexandria, in accordance with the cruising arrangements. At
Alexandria were two battle cruisers, *Inflexible* (flag) and *Indefatigable*,
two armoured cruisers, *Warrior* and *Black Prince*, four light cruisers and
thirteen destroyers. Rear-Admiral Troubridge, flying his flag in the
armoured cruiser *Defence*, with the destroyer *Grampus*, was at Durazzo
in the Adriatic in accordance with Admiralty orders. There also were
the French cruiser *Edgar Quinet* and the German light cruiser *Breslau*.
These vessels represented the various powers supporting the international conference then assembled at Scutari for the purpose of settling
the affairs of Albania.

The battle cruiser *Indomitable* was at Malta, where her annual refit
had just begun, a point to remember in relation to the sequel. The
armoured cruiser *Duke of Edinburgh* was also at Malta, where her annual refit had just been completed. The *Goeben*, flagship of Admiral
Souchon, was then at the Austrian port of Pola, where she had been
refitted, and the *Breslau* (as it has been said) was also in the Adriatic at
Durazzo.

Immediately upon receiving the preliminary telegram of warning on 27th July, I sent instructions to the Admiral Superintendent
at Malta to take all requisite precautions against attack. Ships at Malta
were to be prepared for sea, coal and stores for the fleet were to be
in readiness. A telegram was sent to Rear-Admiral Troubridge at Durazzo to take all requisite precautions against attack. The fleet sailed
from Alexandria on the 28th July.

On 29th July the fleet arrived at Malta. By the afternoon of Satur-

THE ARMOURED CRUISER *DEFENCE*,

day, 1st August, the fleet was in every respect ready for service.

Late in the evening of 29th July I received the warning telegram. On the same date the Admiralty recalled the *Defence*, flagship of Rear-Admiral Troubridge, and the *Grampus* from Durazzo to Malta. On 30th July, in accordance with Admiralty instructions, the P. and O. s.s. *Osiris* was ordered to bring British troops from Scutari to Malta. The *Osiris* was subsequently converted into an auxiliary cruiser.

At eight o'clock on the evening of 30th July, I received the telegram from the Admiralty indicating the political situation and containing my instructions. The communication is summarised in the *Official History of the War: Naval Operations*, by Sir Julian Corbett (Vol. 1), as follows:—

> Admiral Sir Berkeley Milne was informed of the general situation and what he was to do in the case of war. Italy would probably be neutral, but he (Admiral Milne) was not to get seriously engaged with the Austrian Fleet till her (Italy's) attitude was declared.

Sir Julian Corbett's summary of my instructions is sufficiently accurate so far as it goes. The phrase "what he was to do in the case of war," however, may not be clearly understood by the public. As commander-in-chief, I had in my possession written instructions given to me by the Admiralty. It was in the discretion of the Admiralty to direct me to proceed in accordance with those instructions, or to telegraph new orders varying them. In the event of my receiving no new orders, the written instructions stood. It is, of course, conceivable that circumstances might arise in which an admiral's judgment of what ought to be done would conflict with his orders. As the contingency did not, in fact, occur in my own case, there is no need to discuss the point. I wish to make it quite clear from the beginning that the question whether the dispositions ordered by the Admiralty would in all cases have been my dispositions had they been left to my discretion, does not arise.

Sir Julian Corbett proceeds as follows:

> His (Admiral Sir Berkeley Milne's) first task, he was told, should be to assist the French in transporting their African Army, and this he could do by taking up a covering position, and endeavouring to bring to action any fast German ship, particularly the *Goeben*, which might try to interfere with the operation. He was further told not to be brought to action in this stage against

57

superior forces unless it was in a general engagement in which the French forces were taking part.

Reference to the map of the Mediterranean will make clear the strategic position. In the Western Mediterranean the French Fleet was to protect the passage of the French African Army from the ports of Algeria to Toulon. In the Eastern Mediterranean were the *Goeben* and *Breslau*, immediately dangerous; the Austrian Fleet, a potential danger; and the Italian Fleet, doubtfully neutral. Between the Western and the Eastern Mediterranean open two gates; one, the narrow Strait of Messina, the other, the wide channel between Cape Bon on the African coast and Marsala in Sicily. Midway in the channel are placed Malta, the headquarters of the British Fleet, and, further west, the Island of Pantellaria.

The fleet under my command, therefore, was placed between the French Fleet and hostile intervention from the Eastern sea. There were two powers to consider, Austria and Italy; and two German ships to watch, one of which, the *Goeben*, was faster than any other vessel of the same class in the Mediterranean. For all purposes, the force at my disposal consisted of three battle cruisers, four armoured cruisers, four light cruisers and small craft.

On 31st July, I informed the Admiralty that I considered it necessary to concentrate all my available forces, and that I could not at first provide protection to trade in the Eastern Mediterranean. Sir Julian Corbett (*Official History*, 1), states with regard to my dispositions at this time:—

> Considering it unsafe to spread his cruisers for the protection of the trade routes, he contented himself with detaching a single light cruiser, the *Chatham* (Captain Drury-Lowe), to watch the south entrance of the Strait of Messina.

The obvious inference to be drawn from this passage is unfortunate. The disposition of cruisers was not a question of safe or unsafe, nor whether the commander-in-chief was "contented" or not. It was a question of strategic and tactical requirements, whose fulfilment was approved by the Board of Admiralty. Moreover, Sir Julian Corbett is in error in stating that the *Chatham* was despatched on 30th July. She did not leave Malta until 2nd August.

On 31st July, *Defence* (flag of rear-admiral) and *Grampus* arrived at Malta from Durazzo. On the same day, in accordance with Admiralty orders, the *Black Prince* was ordered to Marseilles to embark

THE ARMOURED CRUISER *Black Prince*

Earl Kitchener. The order was cancelled on 2nd August, and the *Black Prince* returned to Malta, arriving there on 3rd August.

On Saturday, 1st August, the Admiralty ordered the Examination Service to be put in force. Instructions were given to get the boom defence at Malta into position. By this date the whole fleet was concentrated at Malta.

On Sunday, 2nd August, I received information that the *Goeben* had been coaling at Brindisi on the previous day. The Admiralty informed me that the situation was very critical. Later in the day I received from the Admiralty instructions summarised in the *Official History* (1), as follows:—

Then, in the afternoon, came further orders which overrode the disposition he had decided on. Informing him that Italy would probably remain neutral, the new instructions directed that he was to remain at Malta himself, but to detach two battle cruisers to shadow the *Goeben*, and he was also to watch the approaches to the Adriatic with his cruisers and destroyers.

In accordance with these instructions, Rear-Admiral Troubridge left Malta the same evening with the battle cruisers *Indomitable* and *Indefatigable*, the three armoured cruisers, *Defence, Warrior, Duke of Edinburgh*, the light cruiser *Gloucester*, and eight destroyers.

The two battle cruisers were attached to the rear-admiral's squadron in accordance with the Admiralty instructions "to detach two battle cruisers to shadow the *Goeben*." The rest of the rear-admiral's force, in accordance with the Admiralty instructions, was ordered to watch the mouth of the Adriatic. Thus Rear-Admiral Troubridge left Malta with two separate forces, each allotted to a particular purpose by the Admiralty. The light cruiser *Chatham* went to search for the German ships in the Strait of Messina. Four destroyers went to patrol the Malta Channel.

CHAPTER 4

The French Dispositions

Upon the same evening, Sunday, 2nd August, I received permission from the Admiralty to communicate with the French Senior Officer. All attempts to communicate with him by wireless having failed, on the following (Monday) evening, I despatched the *Dublin* light cruiser to Bizerta with a letter addressed to the French admiral. It will be observed that upon the very eve of war, it had proved impossible to make any arrangements with the French Naval Forces, with which I had been instructed to work, and hostile interference with which I had been instructed to prevent. It is stated in the *Official History* (1), that:—

> The fact was, there had been a delay in getting the fleet to sea. By the time-table of the war plan it should have been covering the Algerian coasts by August 1, but so anxious, it is said, were the French to avoid every chance of precipitating a conflict, that sailing orders were delayed till the last possible moment. . . . Whatever the real cause, it was not until daybreak on August 3rd that Admiral de Lapeyrère put to sea, with orders 'to watch the German cruiser *Goeben* and protect the transport of the French African troops'.

But of these matters I was necessarily ignorant at the time. I knew nothing of the French naval dispositions, except that, in whatever they consisted, it was my duty to assist in protecting the transport of the French African Army. I was not informed of the dispositions of Admiral de Lapeyrère; I received no reply to wireless calls; and on Monday, 3rd August, I despatched the light cruiser *Dublin* to Bizerta, carrying a letter for the French admiral at that port.

As the *Official History* records, Admiral Boué de Lapeyrère put to sea on the same day at 4 a.m. The French Fleet was formed into three squadrons; the first consisting of six battleships of the *Danton* type, three armoured cruisers and a flotilla of twelve destroyers; the second consisting of six battleships, three armoured cruisers and a flotilla of twelve destroyers; the third consisting of four older battleships. Thus, for covering the passage of their African Army from Algeria to Toulon, there was provided a force of sixteen battleships, six armoured cruisers and twenty-four destroyers.

At the moment it sailed from Toulon:—

Germany had not yet declared war, the attitude of Italy remained doubtful, and it was quite unknown whether Great Britain would come into the war or not. (*Official History*, 1.)

CHAPTER 5

First Meeting with "Goeben" and "Breslau"

I now return to the events of Sunday, 2nd August. As already stated, on the evening of that day Rear-Admiral Troubridge sailed for the entrance to the Adriatic with two battle cruisers, three ships of the First Cruiser Squadron, the light cruiser *Gloucester* and eight destroyers; and later in the day I received information that the *Goeben* had been coaling at Brindisi.

At 5.12 p.m. the *Chatham* (Captain Sidney R. Drury-Lowe), had sailed from Malta with instructions to search for the *Goeben* in the Strait of Messina, and subsequently to join the rear-admiral's squadron.

Four destroyers were patrolling the Malta Channel. My force at Malta was thus reduced to the battle cruiser *Inflexible* (flag), two light cruisers and small craft. According to Admiralty instructions, the *Black Prince*, then on her way to Marseilles to embark Earl Kitchener, was recalled to Malta, where she arrived early on Monday, 3rd August.

On Monday, 3rd August, at 4 a.m. I received further instructions from the Admiralty. These are described by Sir Julian Corbett (*Official History*, 1), as follows:—

> About 1 a.m. on August 3rd, to give further precision to their orders, the Admiralty directed that the watch on the mouth of the Adriatic was to be maintained, but that the *Goeben* was the main objective, and she was to be shadowed wherever she went.

Sir Julian Corbett's comment on his version of the telegram is that:—

> Taking this as a repetition of the previous order which instruct-

Light Cruiser HMS *Gloucester*

ed him to remain near Malta himself. Admiral Milne stayed where he was and left the shadowing to Admiral Troubridge.

Here, again, the implication is inaccurate. Sir Julian Corbett implies that I was acting upon an assumption. Although, as he states, Sir Julian Corbett had access to all telegrams, and therefore he must have read my telegram to the Admiralty of the previous day (2nd August), Sir Julian Corbett neither mentions the telegram nor the fact that in the telegram I expressly submitted to their Lordships that my tactical dispositions required my remaining at Malta for the time being.

The Admiralty reply of the following day was, therefore, both a definite confirmation of my proposed dispositions together with additional instructions concerning them; and I acted, not upon an assumption but, upon orders. These instructions were of the greatest moment. The significant clause was ". . . but *Goeben* is your objective." That order clearly indicated that two immediate objects were to be pursued simultaneously: the watch upon Austria and Italy in the Adriatic, and the watch upon the *Goeben*; and that, of the two, the watch upon the *Goeben* was the more important.

There were also to be fulfilled the earlier instructions: that I was to protect the transport of the French African Army, and to avoid being brought to action by superior forces. The order to protect the French transports was, in fact, covered by the order to watch Italy, Austria and the two German ships. The contingency of being confronted by superior forces, did it occur, must have involved the subordination of all other considerations, for the only way of avoiding action is to retreat.

At 4 a.m. on that Monday morning, 3rd August, I received the Admiralty instructions. At the same time, although I knew nothing of it, the French Fleet sailed from Toulon for the Algerian coast.

At 7 a.m., the *Chatham* reported that neither the *Goeben* nor the *Breslau* was in the Strait of Messina. At the same time, I received information that *Goeben* and *Breslau* had been sighted early on the previous (Sunday) morning off Cape Trion, the southern horn of the Gulf of Taranto, heading south-west. It therefore appeared that the two German ships had escaped from the Adriatic. In order both to maintain the watch on the Adriatic and to find *Goeben* and *Breslau*, at about 8.30 a.m. I ordered Rear-Admiral Troubridge, whose squadron was then about midway between Cape Spartivento, Italy, and Cape Passero, Sicily, to send the light cruiser *Gloucester* and the eight destroyers to the mouth of the Adriatic, while the rest of his squadron was to pass south of Sicily and to the westward. The light cruiser *Chatham* was ordered to pass westward along the north coast of Sicily. The light cruisers *Dublin* and *Weymouth* were set to watch the Malta Channel. These dispositions were made in case the German ships should endeavour to pass westward, and they were reported to the Admiralty.

At 1.30 p.m. I made further dispositions. Rear-Admiral Troubridge was instructed to proceed to the mouth of the Adriatic with the First Cruiser Squadron to support the *Gloucester* and the destroyers there, and *Black Prince* was ordered to rejoin the Cruiser Squadron. The two battle cruisers *Indomitable* and *Indefatigable* were ordered to proceed through the Malta Channel and thence westward to search for *Goeben*, in accordance with the original Admiralty instructions allocating these two ships for that purpose. At the same time the Senior Naval Officer at Gibraltar was requested to keep a close watch for *Goeben* and *Breslau* in case they passed the Strait.

At 5 p.m., as I had failed to establish communication with the French either at Toulon or Bizerta, I despatched the light cruiser *Dublin* to Bizerta, with a letter to the French admiral. I did not, of course, know that by that time the French Fleet, steaming at 12 knots, had been at sea for eleven hours. It appears that the British Admiralty were also ignorant of the sailing of the French Fleet, for it is stated in the *Official History* (1), that "organised connection between the British and French Admiralties had not yet been established." The Admiralty were, therefore, anxious lest the two German ships should escape into the Atlantic. There was never the least suggestion that they might escape elsewhere. My own impression that the Germans would turn westward was confirmed by a report that a German collier was waiting at Majorca.

At 6.30 p.m. in *Inflexible*, I left Malta to take up a watching position in the Malta Channel, together with the light cruiser *Weymouth*, the torpedo-gunboat *Hussar* and three destroyers. At 8.30 p.m. I received instructions from the Admiralty to send two battle cruisers to Gibraltar at high speed to prevent the *Goeben* from leaving the Mediterranean. *Indomitable* and *Indefatigable* were already on their way westward, and they were ordered to proceed at 22 knots to Gibraltar. The Chatham, which was then rounding Sicily, and which had nothing to report, was ordered to Malta to coal.

On Tuesday, 4th August, then, the position was as follows: *Inflexible* (flag), with *Weymouth* and small craft, was patrolling the Malta Channel; Rear-Admiral Troubridge, with the First Cruiser Squadron,

S. M. Panzerkreuzer Goeben
(Türkischer Name: „Sultan Jawus Selim").

was about midway between Malta and the mouth of the Adriatic, on his way to reinforce the *Gloucester* and the destroyers; the light cruiser *Dublin* had gone to Bizerta, with a letter for the French admiral; *Chatham* was coaling in Malta; and the two battle cruisers. *Indomitable*, Captain Francis W. Kennedy (in command). *Indefatigable*, Captain Charles F. Sowerby, were steaming westward at 22 knots.

Where were the *Goeben* and *Breslau?* No one knew. At 7 a.m. on Monday, the *Chatham* had reported they were not in the Strait of Messina. It was now Tuesday. The fact was, they had passed the Strait during the night of Sunday 2nd—Monday 3rd, ahead of the *Chatham*.

At 8.30 a.m. on Tuesday, 4th August, I received information that Bona had been bombarded by the German ships.

At 9.32 a.m. *Indomitable* and *Indefatigable*, off Bona, on the Algerian coast, sighted the *Goeben* and *Breslau*, which were steering to the eastward.

> The *Goeben* was seen at once to alter course to port, and Captain Kennedy altered to starboard in order to close, but the *Goeben* promptly turned away, and in a few minutes the two ships were passing each other on opposite courses at 8,000 yards. Guns were kept trained fore and aft, but neither side saluted, and after passing, Captain Kennedy led round in a wide circle and proceeded to shadow the *Goeben*, with his two ships on either quarter. The *Breslau* made off to the northward and disappeared, and early in the afternoon could be heard calling up the Cagliari wireless stations. (*Official History*, 1.)

Had a state of war then existed, it is probable there would have been a very different end to that meeting.

At 10.30 a.m. *Dublin* arrived at Bizerta, and at my orders she left at once to join *Indomitable* in shadowing the German ships, which were steering eastward, on a course lying north of the Sicilian coast, towards Messina. During the afternoon, *Dublin* joined *Indomitable* and *Indefatigable* at a point north of Bizerta. In the meantime, *Goeben* and *Breslau*, steaming at their utmost speed, were drawing away from the British battle cruisers, which presently lost sight of the German ships. The *Dublin* picked them up about 5 p.m., and kept them in sight until nearly 10 p.m., when she lost them off the Cape San Vito, on the north coast of Sicily, and turned back to rejoin the battle cruisers. The *Goeben* had recently been refitted at Pola, while *Indomitable* had only just been docked for repair when the warning telegram arrived.

During the day *Inflexible* (flag), with a division of destroyers, keeping within visual signalling distance of Castille (Malta), waited in the Malta Channel for information and instructions from the Admiralty. At 8.15 p.m., as already stated, I received information from the French admiral at Bizerta that the *Goeben* had bombarded Bona and that the *Breslau* had bombarded Philippeville, on the Algerian coast. What had happened (as we now know), was that the German vessels, upon leaving Messina on the night of 2nd-3rd August, made a descent upon Bona and Philippeville in order to interfere with the transport of the Eastern Division of the French XIXth Army Corps. According to the *Official History* (1), Admiral Souchon, at 6 p.m. on the 3rd August, learned that war had been declared, but he received no orders until midnight, when he was instructed to proceed with *Goeben* and *Breslau* to Constantinople. Sir Julian Corbett writes:

> Long afterwards, it became known that on the following day (4th August) the *Kaiser* informed the Greek Minister that an alliance had been concluded between Germany and Turkey, and that the German warships in the Mediterranean were to join the Turkish Fleet and act in concert.

That is an affair of diplomacy upon which I make no comment. It is certain at least that I received no information of any such arrangement, nor, according to the *Official History*, had the British authorities any knowledge of that most momentous treaty. All that we knew in the Mediterranean was that the two German ships steered eastward on the 4th August. Germany was then at war with France, but not with England.

At 5 p.m. on 4th August, about the time when the two battle cruisers lost sight of the *Goeben*, I received authority from the Admiralty to engage the German vessels should they attack the French transports. The occasion did not arise, and the order was cancelled in the subsequent telegram received two hours later, informing me that the British ultimatum presented to Germany would expire at midnight.

CHAPTER 6

New Dispositions

At 6 p.m. on the same day, Tuesday, 4th August, I received a telegram from the Admiralty which seriously altered the strategic situation. I was informed that Italy had declared strict neutrality, which was to be rigidly respected, and that no ship of war was to pass within six miles of the Italian coast. The effect of the order was to bar the Strait of Messina, presumably to both belligerents, certainly to British ships. If the *Goeben* and *Breslau* entered the Strait, they could not be followed. They might break back westward or they might turn south through the Strait, and then either turn eastward to the Adriatic, or west through the channel between Africa and Sicily.

In these new circumstances I ordered *Chatham* and *Weymouth* to patrol the channels between the African coast and Pantellaria Island and between Pantellaria Island and the coast of Sicily, in case the German ships should turn south; while, further north, *Indomitable* and *Indefatigable*, and, later, *Dublin* patrolled between Sicily and Sardinia, in case the German ships should turn west again.

At 7 p.m. I received a telegram from the Admiralty informing me that the British ultimatum to Germany would expire at midnight, and that no acts of war should be committed before that hour.

It was now necessary to make new dispositions in accordance with my orders. The neutrality of Italy having been declared, I was relieved of responsibility with regard to the Italian Fleet. But it was still of course necessary to watch the Adriatic, both in case the German ships tried to enter that sea and in case the Austrian Fleet sailed. But my first duty was the protection of the French transports from the *Goeben* and the *Breslau*.

Now the *Goeben* had shown herself to be at least three knots faster than the British battle cruisers. The superiority in speed of the enemy necessarily governed all my dispositions. For the benefit of the lay reader it should here be explained that it is useless to try to overtake a ship which is faster than her pursuer. The chase merely continues until fuel is exhausted. Therefore, in order to catch a ship which is superior in speed to her pursuers, it is necessary that the faster ship should be intercepted by crossing her course. That manoeuvre was performed by *Indomitable* and *Indefatigable* on Tuesday, 4th August, when they were at one time within 8,000 yards of *Goeben*.

That pursuing ships must be so disposed as to cut off the faster ship pursued, is an elementary maxim in tactics which the author of the *Official History* strangely ignores.

In disposing my forces to prevent the *Goeben* and *Breslau* going westward, it was therefore necessary to arrange, not to chase but, to intercept, the enemy. At any moment the Germans might try to break westwards, in which case there were three courses open to them. They might (1) pass north of Corsica; or (2) through the Strait of Bonifacio between Corsica and Sardinia; or (3) south of Sardinia between Sardinia and the African coast. I considered that the German ships would avoid both the north of Corsica and the Strait of Bonifacio, for fear of French cruisers, destroyers and submarines. In all probability they would, therefore, try to pass south of Sardinia, and thence to Majorca, where a German collier was waiting at Palma.

In these circumstances, Rear-Admiral Troubridge was ordered, on Tuesday, 4th August, to detach *Gloucester* to watch the southern end of the Strait of Messina, into which, it will be remembered, British ships of war were forbidden to go. Rear-Admiral Troubridge, with four armoured cruisers and eight destroyers was to continue to watch the mouth of the Adriatic. The two battle cruisers (except *Gloucester*) and three destroyers were ordered to join my flag off Pantellaria Island at 11 a.m. on the following day, 5th August. These dispositions were communicated to the Admiralty at 8.30 p.m. 4th August.

At fifteen minutes past one, 5th August, on the night of 4th-5th August, I received the order to commence hostilities against Germany. I was then in the Malta Channel, and left at once in *Inflexible*, with three destroyers. At about 11 a.m. on 5th August, *Inflexible* (flag). *Indomitable, Indefatigable, Dublin, Weymouth, Chatham* and three destroyers were assembled off Pantellaria Island, midway in the channel between the African coast and Sicily. *Dublin* was sent back to Malta, there to coal and thence to proceed with two destroyers to join Rear-Admiral Troubridge at the mouth of the Adriatic. *Indomitable* and three destroyers went into Bizerta to coal. *Inflexible* (flag) with *Indefatigable*, *Chatham* and *Weymouth*, patrolled on a line northward from Bizerta, being thus disposed to intercept the German ships should they attempt to escape westwards.

At 5 p.m. on Wednesday, 5th August, the German ships were reported to be coaling at Messina.

CHAPTER 7

The "Official" Version

It is at this point in the series of events, as related in the *Official History*, that the following comment is made by the official historian. After quoting from my despatch to the Admiralty, Sir Julian Corbett observes:—

> Nevertheless, he had left the line of attack from Messina open, but, *apart from this serious defect in his dispositions*, (my italics—A. B. M.), they were in accordance with his original instructions. The order that the French transports were to be his first care had not been cancelled, though, in fact, there was now no need for him to concern himself with their safety. (*Official History*, 1.)

I do not propose to discuss my dispositions with Sir Julian Corbett; but I would observe that the official historian states that, in making them, I had departed from my original instructions, and that the result of that departure was a "serious defect." I do not understand what Sir Julian means when he asserts that the line of attack from Messina was left open, nor does he explain his meaning. But I affirm that there was, in fact, no departure from my instructions; and that, as Sir Julian Corbett must be aware, my dispositions were approved by the Admiralty in all respects. Yet we have this extraordinary circumstance, that the Admiralty, having had submitted to them Sir Julian Corbett's statement, allowed it to be published, with what is virtually their approval.

Sir Julian adds that there was no longer any need for me to concern myself with the safety of the French transports. Here the implication is that I knew, and also that the Admiralty knew, the movements of the French Fleet, and that either my original instructions should have been cancelled, or that I should have disobeyed them. Here, again, the Admiralty allowed the publication of what is, in fact, a totally false implication; and which is indeed virtually contradicted by the historian himself; for, after interpolating a description of the rapid and unexpected changes in the disposition of the French naval forces, which were not understood at the time by the British authorities, and which were unknown to me. Sir Julian Corbett proceeds to remark that the reason for my own dispositions "was clearly a belief that the Germans might still have an intention to attack the French convoys, and so long as this was a practical possibility, the Admiral could scarcely disregard his strict injunctions to protect them." (*Official History*, 1.) The historian goes on to describe the position and the feelings of Admiral Souchon and the officers and men of the *Goeben* and *Breslau*, then coaling at Messina, adding, what is perfectly true, that "all this was in the dark, when Admiral Milne, feeling bound by his instructions that the '*Goeben*' was his objective,' made his last dispositions to prevent her escape to the northward."

Sir Julian Corbett would seem to consider, as he certainly implies, that a flag-officer may obey or disobey, according to his fancy, the orders he receives from the Admiralty.

While such a misapprehension might naturally be entertained by a civilian, it cannot possibly exist at the Admiralty; and I am, therefore, at a loss to understand on what principle the Admiralty sanctioned the publication of these passages. The historian further implies that it was, in any case, a mistake to take measures to prevent the *Goeben* and *Breslau* from escaping "northward." Again, that may be the opinion of Sir Julian Corbett; but, again, it cannot possibly be the opinion of the Admiralty, for their Lordships both ordered and subsequently approved that disposition of forces. It was a disposition which, at the time, I considered to be the best disposition, nor do I now perceive what in the circumstances would have been a better strategical distribution. Nor does Sir Julian Corbett suggest one.

Chapter 8

"Goeben" and "Breslau" at Messina

I return to the sequence of the events of Wednesday, 5th August, when *Inflexible* (flag) with *Indefatigable* and *Weymouth* were patrolling the passage between the African coast and the south coast of Sicily. *Indomitable* and three destroyers had gone to Bizerta to coal. *Chatham*, which had captured a German collier, was ordered to take her into Bizerta and coal. *Dublin* was coaling at Malta, and was ordered to proceed thence with three destroyers to join the rear-admiral's squadron at the mouth of the Adriatic. *Gloucester* was watching the southern end of the Strait of Messina.

At midday I received a report that the Austrian Battle Fleet was cruising outside Pola, in the Adriatic. It should be borne in mind that, at this time, the neutrality of Austria was in doubt.

At 2 p.m. I received a telegram from the Admiralty informing me that Austria-Hungary had not declared war against France or Great Britain, and instructing me to continue to watch the mouth of the Adriatic, so that the Austrian Fleet should not emerge unobserved, and that the two German ships should be prevented from entering the Adriatic. It should here be remembered that the numerical and potential superiority of the Austrian Fleet over the British Fleet made the attitude of Austria of supreme moment, a point wholly ignored in the *Official History*.

At 5 p.m. (Wednesday, 5th August) I received a report from *Gloucester* that, judging by wireless signals intercepted, the *Goeben* appeared to be at Messina. It should here be mentioned that on the preceding day I had learned that the *General*, a German mail steamer, had landed passengers at Messina and was remaining at the disposition of the *Goeben*, It was probable, therefore, that *Goeben*, *Breslau* and *General* were all at Messina. A further report to the same effect was received a little later.

At 7 p.m. I received information from the Admiralty that mines had been laid in the Dardanelles (they had been laid before I passed the Straits in June), and that the Dardanelles lights had been extinguished. Had there been any conjecture that the *Goeben* would try to pass the Dardanelles, it would have been weakened by the information that mines had been laid and lights extinguished. But, in fact, there was no such conjecture. According to the *Official History*, it seems that the German admiral himself was in a state of painful irresolution.

> According to Admiral von Tirpitz, when on August 3 news was received of the alleged alliance with Turkey, orders were sent to Admiral Souchon to attempt to break through to the Dardanelles. On August 5 the German Embassy at Constantinople reported that, in view of the situation there, it was undesirable for the ships to arrive for the present. Thereupon the orders for the Dardanelles were cancelled, and Admiral Souchon, who was then coaling at Messina, was directed to proceed to Pola or else break into the Atlantic. Later in the day, however, Austria, in spite of the pressure that was being put upon her from Berlin to declare war, protested she was not in a position to help with her fleet. In these circumstances it was thought best to give Admiral Souchon liberty to decide for himself which line of escape to attempt, and he then chose the line of his first instructions."
> (*Official History*, 1.)

★★★★★★

According to Major Mélas, private secretary to King Constantine of Greece, the existence of the treaty was known in Greece.

> On 4th August, 1914, the *Kaiser* sent for our minister at Berlin and told him that he might officially inform King Constantine that an alliance had been definitely concluded on that day between Germany and Turkey, and gave him to understand, moreover, that certainly Bulgaria, and perhaps Roumania, would range themselves on the side of the Central Powers. (*Ex-King Constantine and the War*. George M. Mélas. Hutchinson, 1920.)

★★★★★★

If the account of Grand-Admiral von Tirpitz, cited by Sir Julian Corbett, be accurate, it will be observed that the whole situation turned upon the conclusion between Germany and Turkey of the secret treaty, which, according to Sir Julian Corbett, was not known to the British Government until "long afterwards." Again assuming von Tirpitz's account to be accurate, it would be interesting to learn what, in the view of Sir Julian Corbett—even if he had known on 5th August, 1914, the circumstances which he relates in his history, and which he states were unknown to the authorities—would have been the correct disposition of the British Fleet remedying the "serious defect" he describes.

Having received no news of the German ships during the night of 5th-6th August, at 6.30 a.m. on Thursday, 6th August, proceeding upon the assumption that they were at Messina, I began a sweep to the eastward, north of Sicily, with *Inflexible* (flag), *Indefatigable* and *Weymouth*. If the *Goeben*, after coaling at Messina, had left the Strait by the north entrance, she would be signalled by my squadron at about 6 p.m. By 4.40 p.m. I had received no report of the departure of the *Goeben* from Messina. That she had not escaped westwards, I knew. She might have gone north, but, considering it improbable that she would take that course, I determined to close the northern entrance to the Strait of Messina. The squadron was disposed accordingly. *Chatham* was ordered to proceed at 20 knots to Milazzo Point, off Messina, and was informed of the position which would be occupied by the two battle cruisers and *Weymouth* at midnight.

These dispositions had scarcely been made when, half an hour later, the *Gloucester*, which was watching the southern entrance to the Strait, reported that the *Goeben* was coming out of the Strait of Messina, the *Breslau* following her one mile astern, steering eastward. The position was then as follows: If *Goeben* and *Breslau* attempted to enter the Adriatic, Rear-Admiral Troubridge, with the First Cruiser Squadron and ten destroyers, would prevent them; if the German ships, followed by *Gloucester*, escaped her in the night and turned westwards, my squadron of battle cruisers must be so placed as to intercept them. As my instructions strictly forbade me to enter the Strait of Messina, I was obliged, in order to take up the requisite position, to come down the west coast of Sicily. With *Inflexible* (flag). *Indefatigable*, *Weymouth* and *Chatham* (recalled) I accordingly proceeded to round the west coast of Sicily.

Further reports from *Gloucester*, which was pursuing the German ships, stated that they were steering eastward, then north-eastward. I therefore continued on my course to Malta, in order to coal there and to continue the chase, arriving at noon on Friday, 7th August. *Chatham* was then ordered to patrol off Milazzo, in case *Goeben* and

Breslau should turn back and escape through the Strait of Messina northward.

In the meantime, at 11 p.m. on the night of Thursday, 6th August, I had received a telegram from the Admiralty countermanding previous instructions and ordering me, if the *Goeben* went south, *to follow her through the Strait of Messina*. Unfortunately, by the time the new instructions reached me, it was too late to fulfil them. I was then off Maritimo, the west coast of Sicily, and to return to Messina would have involved traversing two sides of a triangle, instead of the one which I had still to traverse, as a reference to the chart will show; or, as it stated in the *Official History* 1:—

> Unfortunately, it (the telegram) did not come to hand till midnight, too late for the admiral to modify the movement to which he was committed.

In the *Official History* occurs the following account of the dispositions of the German ships, taken from Ludwig's *Die Fahrten der Goeben und der Breslau:*—

> Admiral Souchon's intention, as his one chance of escape, was to steer a false course until nightfall, so as to give the impression he was making back to join the Austrians in the Adriatic, and as his reserve ammunition had been sent to Pola, this was probably the original intention before the intervention of Great Britain rendered that sea nothing but a trap. The orders he issued were that the *Goeben* would leave at 5 p.m. at seventeen knots; the *Breslau* would follow five miles astern, closing up at dark; while the *General*, sailing two hours later, would keep along the Sicilian coast and make, by a southerly track, for Santorin, the most southerly island of the Archipelago. The two cruisers, after steering their false course till dark, would make for Cape Matapan (south of Greece), where, as we have seen, a collier had been ordered to meet them. In accordance with this plan, Admiral Souchon, the moment he sighted the *Gloucester*, altered course to port so as to keep along the coast of Calabria (Italy) outside the six-mile limit. (*Official History*, 1.)

Sir Julian Corbett, in preparing his material, had before him the orders of the German and French admirals, as well as those of the British admiral; he also knew the actual dispositions and movements from day to day, the objects with which they were made, and the actual results obtained. He seems, perhaps unconsciously, to ignore the fact that the orders and the dispositions of French and German ships were unknown at the time both to the Admiralty and to the British commander-in-chief.

For instance, Sir Julian Corbett, referring to my dispositions, proceeds to affirm that:—

> My idea was that Admiral Troubridge, with his squadron and his eight destroyers, besides two more which were being hurried off to him from Malta in charge of the *Dublin*, was strong enough to bar the Adriatic, and that there was still a possibility of the German making back to the westward along the south of Sicily.

Here, again, the implication is clearly that my "idea" was mistaken; and again I have to observe that it was not a question of ideas, but of the best dispositions it was possible to make in the circumstances, dispositions which were demanded by the only known conditions of the problem, and which were approved at every stage by the Admiralty.

CHAPTER 9

Second Meeting with "Goeben" and "Breslau"

To return to the chase of the *Goeben* and *Breslau* so gallantly conducted by Captain W. A. Howard Kelly in *Gloucester*. At 7.30 p.m. on
Thursday, 6th August, the German ships were steering north-east
along the coast of Calabria, between *Gloucester* and the land. As the
dark fell, they were becoming lost to sight; and Captain Kelly, in order to keep them in view and to get them in the light of the moon,
steered inshore to reverse the position. In so doing, he ran well within
range of the *Goeben*, which could have sunk him, and proceeded on
her port quarter.

The *Breslau* then began to pinch him inshore, and Captain Kelly
was obliged to drop back. The *Breslau* steered to cross his bows; Captain Kelly altered course to meet her; and the two ships passed each
other at a distance of 4,000 yards. Captain Kelly, rightly considering
it to be his first duty to follow the *Goeben*, did not open fire. *Breslau*
retreated east-south-eastwards and disappeared. Captain Kelly held on
in chase of *Goeben*. At about two o'clock the *Goeben*, then off the Gulf
of Squillace, also altered course to the southward.

In the meantime, Rear-Admiral Troubridge, who had been patrolling with the First Cruiser Squadron (*Defence*-flag, *Warrior*, *Duke of
Edinburgh*, *Black Prince*) off Cephalonia, on the west coast of Greece,
upon learning that the German ships were steering north-eastward,
went north, in order to engage them off Fano Island, should they attempt to enter the Adriatic. When he learned that the *Goeben* and *Breslau* had altered course to the southward, Rear-Admiral Troubridge,
at midnight on the night of 6th-7th August, turned south to intercept
them. In the *Official History* it is stated that:—

His intention had been to engage the *Goeben* if he could get contact before 6 a.m., since that was the only chance of his being able to engage her closely enough for any prospect of success, and when he found it impossible, he thought it his duty not to risk his squadron against an enemy who, by his superiority in speed and gun-power, could choose his distance and outrange him.

At 4 a.m. on the morning of Friday, 7th August, I received information from Rear-Admiral Troubridge that he had abandoned the chase of the German ships; or, to be more exact, that he had abandoned his intention of intercepting them and bringing them to action.

For his conduct on this occasion Rear-Admiral Troubridge was tried by court-martial and was "fully and honourably" acquitted.

★★★★★★

Sir Julian Corbett quotes the verdict of the Court, thus suggesting that he had access to the records of the court-martial, which was held in secret. Indeed, his whole account of the matter gives the same impression. The papers have been denied to Parliament.

★★★★★★

There is, of course, nothing more to be said on the matter; and my observations upon the episode do not refer to Rear-Admiral Troubridge, but to the account of the episode presented in the *Official History* 1.

It is there stated that Rear-Admiral Troubridge "had received no authority to quit his position, nor any order to support the *Gloucester*". The statement is incorrect. On 3rd August, the rear-admiral had received the Admiralty instructions (already described) to maintain the watch on the Adriatic, and stating, "but *Goeben* is your objective." Nor are the rear-admiral's signals to me, to which Sir Julian Corbett presumably had access, in accordance with Sir Julian's statement.

Sir Julian Corbett proceeds (1) to make the following extraordinary statement:—

Still, he (Rear-Admiral Troubridge) only slowed down, and held on as he was, in expectation that his two battle cruisers would now be sent back to him, with instructions for concerting action.

I do not know why Sir Julian Corbett should attribute that action and that expectation to the rear-admiral. He did not, as the chart (No.

ARMOURED CRUISER HMS *DUKE OF EDINBURGH*

4) published in the *Official History* clearly shows, hold on "as he was," but turned eastward to Zante. Nor is it possible to understand why the rear-admiral should be described as regarding the battle cruisers as "his," when they were no part of his command, and as expecting the arrival of ships which he knew were 300 miles away, a fact which Sir Julian Corbett could have ascertained had he consulted the Admiralty chart accompanying the text of his own *Official History*. Still less is it possible to understand why the Admiralty should have permitted the publication of these blunders.

A little further back in his account of the matter (1), Sir Julian Corbett actually represents Rear-Admiral Troubridge as expecting on the previous Wednesday, 5th August, that "his two battle cruisers would now be returned to him" when the rear-admiral, of course, knew that they were cruising north of Sicily. It has already been explained that the two battle cruisers were at first attached to the rear-admiral's squadron for the sole purpose of shadowing the German ships. Then follows this remarkable passage, in which Rear-Admiral Troubridge is described as entertaining quite inexplicable ideas:—

> Indeed, his impression was that when they (the two battle cruisers) were first attached to his flag it was a preliminary step to the whole command devolving on him. For in the provisional conversations with France it was understood that the British squadron at the outbreak of war would come automatically under the French commander-in-chief—an arrangement which necessarily involved the withdrawal of an officer of Admiral Milne's seniority.

Sir Julian Corbett's reason for attributing this singular view to the rear-admiral can only be conjectured. As a matter of fact, the arrangement between the French and British Governments to which he refers was not signed until 6th August, and I received no copy of it until my arrival at Malta on 10th August. Nor under that agreement was the command to pass to the French admiral until the XlXth Army Corps had been landed in France. But, in any case, it is quite incredible that a flag-officer should be under the "impression" that any strategical dispositions were a "preliminary step to the whole command devolving on him," in the absence of any notification to that effect. Rear-Admiral Troubridge, however, is in a position to defend himself. Sir Julian Corbett, assuming their accuracy, proceeds to imply that I ought to have acted in accordance with a state of things which did not, in fact, exist. Sir Julian writes (1):—

> Admiral Milne, however, took an entirely different view, and still feeling bound by his 'primary object,' began at 7.30 a.m. on August 6 to sweep to the eastward, intending to be in the longitude of Cape San Vito, the north-west point of Sicily, by 6 p.m., 'at which hour,' so he afterwards explained, 'the *Goeben* could have been sighted if she had left Messina,' where he considered she was probably coaling.

The true sequence of events, as already narrated, sufficiently indicates the series of false implications contained in this passage. The main implication is, not only that I was mistaken in every particular, but that the Admiralty were also mistaken. If there is any other inference to be drawn from this part of Sir Julian Corbett's *History*, it is that the forces operating to the north of Messina should have been withdrawn in defiance of all instructions, leaving that way of escape open to the *Goeben*.

At about the time (midnight, 6th-7th August) when Rear-Admiral Troubridge turned south from off Santa Maura to intercept the German ships, the *Dublin* and two destroyers, on the way to join the rear-admiral, sighted, in the moonlight, smoke on the horizon. Captain John Kelly, commanding *Dublin*, had been guided by signals received from his brother, Captain W. A. Howard Kelly, commanding *Gloucester*, then chasing the *Goeben*. At first Captain Kelly, in *Dublin*, took the ship in sight to be *Goeben*. Then the signals from *Gloucester* told him that she must be *Breslau*, and at 4 a.m. he altered course to attack *Goeben* by torpedo.

But Captain John Kelly failed to find *Goeben*, and continued on his course to join the rear-admiral's flag. Captain Howard Kelly, in *Gloucester*, continued his pursuit of the *Goeben*. At about 5.30 a.m. (Friday, 7th August), I signalled to Captain Kelly instructing him gradually to drop astern and to avoid capture. Captain Kelly held on, and at 10.30 a.m. *Breslau* rejoined *Goeben*. At about 1 p.m., *Breslau*, in order to check *Gloucester*, began to drop astern. Captain Kelly, in order to keep *Goeben* in sight, determined to engage *Breslau*, so that either she would be forced to retreat towards *Goeben*, or *Goeben* would be compelled to turn back.

At 1.35 he opened fire, which was returned. Captain Kelly increased speed, brought the enemy on his starboard quarter and continued fire, it is believed with effect. The manoeuvre had the result intended, for the *Goeben* turned 16 points and opened fire, whereupon Captain Kelly broke off the action, retreated, and then continued the chase until the German ships had rounded Cape Matapan. I had ordered Captain Kelly, who was, I knew, getting short of coal, and who ran great risk of capture, to stop pursuit at Cape Matapan and to rejoin the rear-admiral. At 4.40 p.m., then Captain Kelly turned, while the German ships held on through the Cervi Channel, between the southern extremity of Greece and the island of Kithera.

Captain Kelly was highly commended for his action by the Admiralty, and received the honour of the Companionship of the Bath. During the night of 6th-7th August, I had received an offer from the French admiral to place at my disposal a squadron of armoured cruisers. (*Bruix, Latouche-Tréville, Admiral Charner* and cruiser *Jurien de la Gravière*.)

CHAPTER 10

Further Dispositions

At noon on Friday, 7th August—while *Gloucester* was still pursuing *Goeben*—*Inflexible* (flag), *Indefatigable* and *Weymouth* arrived at Malta and coaled. *Chatham* was then patrolling north of Messina. *Indomitable*, which had been coaling at Bizerta, arrived at Malta shortly after the arrival there of the rest of my squadron.

In the *Official History* (1) it is stated that:—

> The *Indomitable* at Bizerta was greatly delayed in coaling, so that it was not until 7 p.m. she was ready to sail, and then she received her orders—but they were not that she should reinforce Admiral Troubridge. (The footnote in *Official History*, referring to the coal supply at Bizerta, is inaccurate. The collier mentioned was sent in by me to supply the fleet.)

Here there is a clear implication on the part of the historian that the *Indomitable* should have been sent to reinforce the rear-admiral in the Adriatic. Again, it is stated that:—

> The *Indomitable* was coming up astern at 21 knots, and when she reached Malta, he (the commander-in-chief) did not send her on, but kept her there till his two other ships had coaled.

Sir Julian Corbett here distinctly implies that the *Indomitable* was kept at Malta without reason. The reasons, however, are contained in the documents to which Sir Julian Corbett had access. There were two reasons. One was that in pursuing the German ships at full speed on 4th August, there occurred boiler defects in *Indomitable*, which made it necessary to spend twelve hours in Malta in repairing them. The other reason was related to that superiority in speed possessed by the *Goeben*, which the official historian ignores. At noon on 7th Au-

BATTLE CRUISER HMS *INDEFATIGABLE*

gust, when *Indomitable* arrived at Malta, *Goeben* was off the southern extremity of Greece, and proceeding eastwards.

Had *Indomitable* (without repairing her boiler defects) been ordered to proceed direct from Bizerta, at the time of her leaving that port on the evening of 6th August, she would have been some 350 miles distant from *Gloucester*, and about 365 miles distant from the German ships. *Goeben* and *Breslau* were then steering towards the Adriatic, where Rear-Admiral Troubridge, with the First Cruiser Squadron was waiting for them. When, later in the evening, I learned that the German ships had turned south, it was necessary to prevent their return westward to attack the French transports. In order to do so, the battle cruiser squadron must be so disposed as to intercept the German ships. As already explained, owing to their superior speed, to attempt to catch them by pursuit was useless.

When upon the afternoon of 7th August, *Goeben* and *Breslau* entered the Cervi Channel, *Indomitable* would have been at least 180 miles distant from *Goeben*, and, supposing *Goeben* to continue to steam at only 15 knots, it would have taken *Indomitable*, steaming at 20 knots, another thirty-six hours to overhaul *Goeben*.

For these reasons, I considered it advisable to keep *Indomitable* with the rest of the Second Battle Cruiser Squadron, a decision which was approved by the Admiralty. But, apart from these considerations, had I sent *Indomitable* to chase *Goeben*, the sequel shows that the only result would have been to run her out of coal at a critical moment when the telegram notifying declaration of war against Austria having been received, it was necessary to concentrate the fleet.

With reference to the dispositions of Rear-Admiral Troubridge on the night of 6th-7th August, it is stated in the *Official History* (1) that:—

> The rear-admiral's destroyers, with scarcely any coal in their bunkers, were all either at Santa Maura or patrolling outside. His intention, as we have seen, had been to seek an engagement only at dusk, but Admiral Milne had ordered him to leave a night action to his destroyers.

In a footnote it is added:—

> Their collier had been ordered to Port Vathi in Ithaca, but the Greek skipper had gone to another port of the same name.

It would be hard to pack more errors in the same number of words.

93

The collier described as going to Port Vathi in Samos—not Ithaca—was the Greek vessel *Petros*, which several days later was taken up by the British Minister at Athens to carry 1,000 tons of coal from the Piraeus. The collier sent by me to supply the destroyers in the Adriatic was the *Vesuvio*, which left Malta at 8 p.m. on 6th August for Port Vathi, Ithaca—not Samos—where she duly arrived at 2 p.m. on the 8th. The rear-admiral was informed of her despatch, but he was evidently ignorant of her arrival, for he continued to report to me difficulties due to deficiency of coal. When, early on the 9th August, *Weymouth* visited Port Vathi, she found that the collier had arrived as arranged.

It is apparently the intention of the whole passage in the *Official History* referring to the lack of coal of the destroyers in the Adriatic, to suggest negligence on my part. The difficulty of obtaining coal was indeed considerable, and necessarily affected the disposition of forces, but not as implied in the *Official History*.

It may here be explained that at noon, on 7th August, I was informed by Rear-Admiral Troubridge that he was supplying destroyers with coal sufficient to enable them to steam to Malta at 15 knots. On the following day, 8th August (to anticipate a little the order of events), *Gloucester* reported that the second division of destroyers was kept at the Ionian Islands for want of coal, and in the evening the rear-admiral informed me that no destroyer had more than 40 tons. As it has been explained, the collier *Vesuvio* had already (2 p.m., 8th August) arrived at Port Vathi, Ithaca, unknown to the rear-admiral. By 9th August three more colliers were on their way to Port Vathi and an ample supply of coal was thus secured.

To return to the events of Friday, 7th August. At 8 p.m. three destroyers were sent to watch the southern end of the Strait of Messina, in case the German ships should return and attempt to pass the Strait. The patrol was maintained until 15th August. As the French squadron of armoured cruisers was patrolling the channel between Cape Bon, on the African coast, and Marsala in Sicily, both the westward lines of retreat were thus effectively watched.

At midnight a report was received that the German mail steamer *General*, after transformation into an armed auxiliary cruiser, had left Messina steering south. The French admiral at Bizerta and all his ships were informed of the report.

BATTLE CRUISER HMS *INDOMITABLE*

CHAPTER 11

The Mistaken Telegram

Before 1 a.m. on the morning of Saturday, 8th August, the Second Battle Cruiser Squadron, *Inflexible* (flag). *Indomitable* and *Indefatigable*, and *Weymouth* having completed with coal, sailed from Malta to search for *Goeben* and *Breslau*, which had been last seen by *Gloucester*, at 5.12 p.m. on the previous evening, steering east at 15 knots through the Cervi Channel, between Cape Malea, the southern extremity of Greece, and the Island of Kithera. At 8.37 a.m., 8th August, information was received that no German ships were at Naples. At 9.15 a.m. *Chatham*, patrolling to the north of Messina, was ordered to proceed southward through the Strait of Messina at 20 knots to Malta, there to coal.

Then occurred an incident which necessarily affected the whole of my dispositions, with the result that the pursuit of the German vessels was checked for twenty-four hours. The actual delay was much longer, as will appear, because the alteration of dispositions involved a considerable divergence of course and a consequent retracing of track.

In the *Official History* the account of the matter is as follows:

Then fortune played another trick, for here he received from the Admiralty a warning, which had been sent out by mistake, that hostilities had commenced against Austria. He could not yet tell whether the *Goeben's* objective might not be Alexandria and our Levant and Eastern trade, but since his last news of the French Fleet was that it would not be free to co-operate with him before the 10th, his *only course seemed to be to turn back and re-concentrate his fleet.* (My italics—A. B. M).

He therefore proceeded to a position 100 miles south-west-ward of Cephalonia so as to prevent the Austrians cutting him off from his base, and ordered Admiral Troubridge to join him.

The *Gloucester* and the destroyers were to do the same, while the *Dublin* and *Weymouth* were left to watch the Adriatic. Later on in the day, (August 8,) he was informed that the alarm was false, but as, at the same time, he was instructed that relations with Austria were critical, he continued his movement for concentration till noon on the 9th. Then came a telegram from the Admiralty to say definitely we were not at war with Austria and that he was to resume the chase.

The official historian here implies that in making the new dispositions, inaccurately described as "turning back," there was a choice of courses to be followed. There was, in fact, no such choice. My written instructions concerning measures to be taken in case of war with Austria were explicit and definite. Either Sir Julian Corbett, in compiling his narrative, had access to copies of those instructions, or he had not. If he had access to them, I am at a loss to understand why he should imply that there was an alternative course, or that any considerations other than my instructions could possibly affect my action. If Sir Julian Corbett did not see my instructions, it is equally difficult to understand why he should have drawn conclusions for which he had no warrant, and why the Admiralty, which were aware of the facts, should have allowed those conclusions to pass.

What actually happened was that at 2 p.m. on Saturday, 8th August, when the squadron was half-way between Sicily and Greece, steering eastward, I received a telegram, ordering hostilities against Austria to be begun at once. Acting instantly upon the instructions provided for that contingency, I proceeded to a position in which I could support Rear-Admiral Troubridge's squadron, then watching the mouth of the Adriatic, and issued orders concentrating the fleet.

In order to execute these dispositions, it was necessary to turn north-westwards, and to steer for a rendezvous 100 miles south-west of Cephalonia, at which the rear-admiral was ordered to join my flag. *Weymouth* was sent to join *Dublin* at the mouth of the Adriatic, and *Chatham* was ordered to join them so soon as she had finished coaling at Malta. *Gloucester* was ordered to convoy destroyers. Thus, at the critical moment of the search for the German vessels, the whole of the light cruiser force was diverted northwards from the line of pursuit.

At 4 p.m., a telegram was received from the Admiralty negativing the previous telegram. The new message being made in a somewhat irregular manner, it could not be accepted as genuine without confirmation, which was accordingly requested. The reply, received at 6 p.m., confirmed the negative telegram. A little later, in a further telegram from the Admiralty, the situation with regard to Austria was described as critical. In these circumstances, it was my duty to continue to act upon my instructions relating to the contingency of war with Austria. It is enough to say, as the *Official History* correctly states, that those instructions involved the concentration of the fleet and consequently the entire abandonment of the pursuit of the German vessels.

★★★★★

Later on in the day, (August 8), he was informed that the alarm was false, but as, at the same time, he was instructed that the relations with Austria were critical, he continued his movement for concentration till noon on the 9th. (*Official History*, 1.)

★★★★★★

At noon on Sunday, 9th August, I received a telegram from the Admiralty stating definitely that Great Britain was not at war with Austria, and instructing me to resume the pursuit of the *Goeben*, Twenty-four hours had thus elapsed since the arrival of the order from the Admiralty to begin hostilities against Austria, compelling me to alter the whole of my dispositions and thus to relinquish the search for the German vessels, which were therefore twenty-four hours steaming further away.

CHAPTER 12

The Search Resumed

When at noon on Sunday, 9th August, I received orders to resume the search, the Second Battle Cruiser Squadron, with *Weymouth*, was off Cephalonia. The light cruisers *Gloucester* and *Chatham* were at Malta, coaling, and *Chatham's* circulating engine was under repair. These ships were ordered to join my flag. Rear-Admiral Troubridge, with the First Cruiser Squadron, *Dublin* and ten destroyers, was instructed to continue to patrol the mouth of the Adriatic. With *Inflexible* (flag), *Indomitable*, *Indefatigable* and *Weymouth*, I proceeded immediately down the west coast of Greece towards Cape Matapan, to search for the German vessels.

In the *Official History* (1), it is stated that:—

The movement involved some risk, since, for the time, it left Admiral Troubridge in the air. . . .

It is an expression I am unable to understand, nor does the official historian explain what other course was possible. Sir Julian Corbett proceeds:—

Since Admiral Milne came down the Greek coast at only 10 knots, presumably to allow his light cruisers to come up, it was not till 8 a.m. on August 10 that he entered the Aegean.

The passage clearly implies that time was lost. That erroneous implication is evidently due to Sir Julian Corbett's ignorance of the tactical problem involved in the superior speed possessed by the *Goeben*, already described. Slow speed was made, not "presumably" in order to enable the light cruisers to rejoin the Second Battle Cruiser Squadron, as Sir Julian Corbett conjectures, but absolutely for that purpose; for the simple reason that to search for ships of superior speed among the

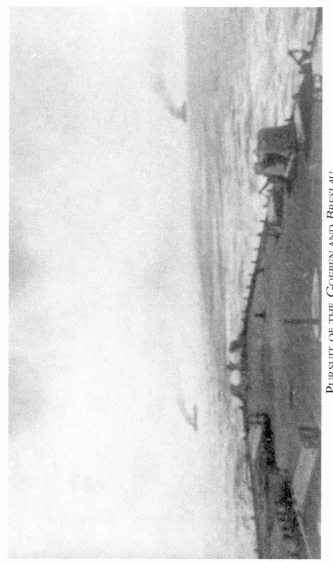

PURSUIT OF THE *GOEBEN* AND *BRESLAU*

islands of the Aegean Sea with battle cruisers alone would have been an insane proceeding. The only chance of catching the German vessels was to discover their position with the swift light cruisers and then to manoeuvre with the battle cruisers to cut them off.

During Sunday, 9th August, I received no reliable information concerning the position of the German vessels. As recorded in the *Official History*, *Goeben* and *Breslau* were in fact at Denusa, a small island at the mouth of the Aegean, at which they arrived on the morning of Saturday, 8th August; and the armed auxiliary steamer *General*, after holding a southern course from Messina, turning north-eastward and passing north of Crete, had arrived at Smyrna on the morning of Sunday, 9th August.

******

Admiral Souchon was actually still at Denusa, waiting to hear that permission to enter the Dardanelles had been negotiated. But not a word could the *General* pass him of any alteration in the situation. (*Official History*, 1.)

******

As the movements and intentions of the German vessels were utterly unknown to me, it was necessary to take measures in accordance with probable contingencies. These were: (1) That the *Goeben* might attempt to take refuge in a Greek port, where Admiral Souchon could rely on the good offices of Greece. (The German admiral was accustomed to use Phalerum in time of peace.) (2) That the *Goeben* might proceed to Salonika to attack that port and thus destroy the Serbian supplies. (3) That she might turn south to attack the south-eastern trade and to destroy British shipping at Alexandria and Port Said. (4) That she might attempt to return westward and to leave the Mediterranean.

Under these conditions it was clearly my duty to try to keep the German ships to the north. Therefore, the battle cruisers must remain in the south-west part of the Aegean until definite information of the positions of the German ships could be obtained.

In accordance with these considerations, the battle cruisers having rounded Cape Malea, the southern extremity of Greece, at 10.55 p.m. on Sunday, 9th August (some fifty-nine hours after *Goeben* and *Breslau* had passed the same point), upon entering the Aegean, were spread twelve miles apart to patrol on a north-easterly course, while *Weymouth* was detached to search the Kithera and Antikithera channels, thence south-east towards Crete, thence north-east to the island of Milo. It will be observed that the rest of the light cruisers—*Gloucester*,

Chatham, Dublin—had not as yet had time to join my flag.

At 9.30 a.m. on Monday, 10th August, wireless signals of the note and code used by the *Goeben* were recognised, but the direction could not be ascertained. In case the *Goeben* might be to the southward of the squadron, course was altered to the south, the ships being spread twelve miles apart. Soon afterwards, signals were heard which seemed to confirm the southerly position of *Goeben*. But at 2.10 p.m. as the signals became weaker, the squadron turned northward again.

In the meantime, *Weymouth* was searching among the islands. At about 6 p.m. *Indefatigable* looked into Milo. *Chatham*, proceeding to Cape Malea, was given her course to search among the islands. Towards dark the three battle cruisers assembled and proceeded in company through the Siphano Channel.

Between 4 a.m. and 5 a.m., on Tuesday, 11th August, the wireless signals of the German armed auxiliary *General* increased in strength; whereupon *Weymouth* was ordered to proceed to examine the Gulf of Smyrna; further instructions to search among the islands were given to *Chatham*; and the battle cruisers, keeping within searchlight signalling distance, were spread to search. At 6 a.m., *Dublin*, sent to join my flag by the rear-admiral, rounded Cape Malea and was sent to Milo Island to coal.

CHAPTER 13

The Escape

It was at 10.30 a.m., on Tuesday, 11th August, that I received the first definite information of the position of the German vessels since the *Gloucester*, upon turning back, had seen *Goeben* and *Breslau* enter the Cervi Channel at 4.40 p.m. on Friday, 7th August. At 10.30 on the morning of the 11th August, then, I received a telegram from Malta informing me that *Goeben* and *Breslau* had arrived at the Dardanelles at nine o'clock on the previous evening, 10th August.

Weymouth was immediately ordered to proceed at full speed to watch the Dardanelles, and, if the German vessels were not to be seen, to pass up to Chanak, hugging the European shore. The battle cruisers proceeded to a position north-west of Psara Island (about the middle of the Aegean Sea) to maintain a watch for the German vessels until their position could be ascertained by the light cruisers. *Chatham* and *Gloucester* were ordered to rejoin flag after dark. *Dublin*, then coaling at Milo Island, was ordered to be ready to pick up and pursue *Goeben* if she came south.

At 3.8 p.m. I received a telegram from the Admiralty stating that *Goeben* and *Breslau* had arrived in the Dardanelles upon the previous evening, and ordering me to establish a blockade of the Dardanelles, an order which was subsequently modified to instructions to keep watch in case the German ships came out.

In the *Official History* (1), it is stated that the order was "to blockade the exit," and there is no mention of the subsequent change to "watch." To blockade involves the stopping and searching of all ships of neutral powers, to which notice must be given beforehand. To watch is a normal operation.

At 5 p.m., Tuesday, 11th August, *Weymouth* arrived off Dardanelles, where she was met by two Turkish torpedo boats, and was greeted by a blank charge fired by one of the forts. She reported that the signal station refused her permission to enter the Straits, and that the guns of the forts on both sides were trained upon her. *Weymouth* was ordered to remain three miles outside the Dardanelles and to report if the enemy, who was at Chanak, came out. The battle cruisers were dispersed upon a patrol whose northern limit was seventeen miles south-west from Tenedos Island. *Chatham* and *Gloucester* were assigned watching positions.

On Wednesday, 12th August, a Turkish military officer came out in a torpedo boat, and at 8 a.m. he informed Captain William D. Church, in command of *Weymouth*, that the *Goeben* and *Breslau* were then at Constantinople and that they had been purchased by the Turkish Government. During the day, I was informed that the *Goeben* had sailed from Chanak for Constantinople at 2 p. m. on the previous day; that the *Breslau* was anchored off Nagara Point; that the *General* (with the *Corcovado*) was at Constantinople; and that all these vessels were flying the German flag.

During Wednesday, 12th August, a close watch was maintained on the Dardanelles, and all steamers were boarded. A Greek destroyer was also watching the Dardanelles. She reported that two Greek cruisers and a destroyer flotilla were at Port Mudros.

At a little past midnight on the night of 12th-18th August, I received orders from the Admiralty to proceed in *Inflexible* (flag) to Malta. Shortly afterwards was received the Admiralty telegram ordering hostilities to be commenced against Austria. At the same time, I received instructions with regard to the ships to be placed under the orders of the French commander-in-chief.

CHAPTER 14

The Sequel

Inflexible (flag), with *Weymouth* and *Dublin,* sailed at 3 a.m. on Thursday, 18th August, and arrived at Malta at 4.45 p.m. on Friday, 14th August. In accordance with my instructions, I made arrangements for turning over the records of the station to Rear-Admiral Garden. According to the agreement concluded between the French and British Governments on the 6th August, the supreme command in the Mediterranean was to pass to the French admiral, while all French ships on all other stations in the world were to come under British officers. As I was of senior rank to the French commander-in-chief in the Mediterranean, Vice-Admiral A. Boué de Lapeyrère, the arrangement was that I should return to England so soon as the French vice-admiral was able to take over the supreme command.

On 18th August, I left Malta in *Inflexible* for Plymouth.

In the *Official History* (1) occur the following comments:—

The outcome of a situation which had been so promising, and which might well have resulted in a success, priceless at the opening of the war, was a severe disappointment. But on his return home the commander-in-chief was able to give explanations of his difficulties and he was exonerated from blame. In view of the instructions which the Admiralty had given him in their anxiety to protect the French transport line and to respect the neutrality of Italy, it is clear that what blame there was could not rest solely on the shoulders of the admiral.

His failure was due, at least in part, to the fact that, owing to the rapid changes in the situation, it was practically impossible for the Admiralty to keep him adequately informed. The sudden pressure on an embryonic staff organisation was more than it could bear, but the fact remains that intelligence essential for forming a correct appreciation of the shifting situation either did not reach him, or reached him too late, and, what was more embarrassing, his original instructions as to his 'primary object' were not cancelled when they were rendered obsolete by the action of the Toulon Fleet.

The student of the true narrative of the course of events will form his own estimate of the justice of Sir Julian Corbett's criticism, in which both the action of the Admiralty and my own conduct are arraigned.

But it is right to observe that when Sir Julian Corbett states that I was "exonerated from blame"; that "what blame there was could not rest solely on the shoulders of the admiral"; and that "his failure was due," etc.; there is a clear implication that a charge was brought against me. There was, of course, no such charge. I was, in fact, privileged to receive the expression of the approval of the Lords Commissioners of the Admiralty; as Sir Julian Corbett must have been well aware, although he omits to mention the circumstance.

On 29th August, 1914, the Admiralty further issued to the Press the following official announcement:—

> The *admiralissimo* of the French Fleet, Rear-Admiral Boué de Lapeyrère, has assumed command of the combined Anglo-French Fleet in the Mediterranean. As a consequence. Admiral Sir Berkeley Milne, Bart., who is senior to this officer, has given over the command of the Mediterranean Fleet and returned home.
>
> The conduct and dispositions of Admiral Sir Berkeley Milne in regard to the German vessels *Goeben* and *Breslau* have been the subject of the careful examination of the Board of Admiralty, with the result that their Lordships have approved the measures taken by him in all respects.

In connection with the whole account of the episode contained in the *Official History*, it is pertinent briefly to recapitulate the tenor of the general instructions received by me from the Admiralty.

The *Goeben* and *Breslau* were to be prevented from interfering with the transport of the French African Army, and from leaving the Mediterranean by the Strait of Gibraltar.

The *Goeben* and *Breslau* were to be prevented from entering the Adriatic.

In case of the emergence from the Adriatic of Austrian ships of war, these vessels were to be watched.

The *Goeben* and *Breslau* were to be prevented from interfering with the trade in the Eastern basin of the Mediterranean.

The possibility that Italy would join Austria and Germany was to be borne in mind.

The neutrality of Italy was to be rigidly respected; no ship of war being permitted to go within six miles of the Italian coast.

In accordance with these instructions, dispositions were made to prevent the German ships from going westward. When they moved eastward, it was necessary to prevent them from again turning westward. When they entered the Aegean Sea, dispositions were made, should they either turn westward, or southward towards the Eastern trade routes and Egypt, to ensure that they would be closely pursued. The possibility was also considered that the German vessels might go to Salonika in order to interfere with the transport of Serbian supplies. It is therefore evident that the purposes indicated in my orders were fulfilled.

CHAPTER 15

Conclusion

Upon my retirement from the Royal Navy in February 1919, the Lords Commissioners of the Admiralty published the following statement in the Press:—

> On the retirement of Admiral Sir Berkeley Milne, it has been brought to the notice of the Board that this officer's professional reputation is stated to have suffered in the opinion of the public owing to its being generally supposed that he did not take up the Command at the Nore—to which he had been appointed before the war—or receive further employment, in consequence of events connected with the escape of the German ships *Goeben* and *Breslau* in 1914. This is not the case. The Admiralty at the time issued an official statement, which remains on record, exonerating Admiral Milne from blame, and intimating that the general dispositions and measures taken by him were fully approved. It has been solely owing to the exigencies of the Service that the admiral has not been further employed.

It will be observed that the *Official History* was published (March 1920) a year after the Admiralty had issued their statement quoted above. During that year, Sir Julian Corbett states that the Admiralty had read the proofs of the book, in which certain alterations had been made in accordance with the suggestions of the Admiralty. These circumstances make it even more difficult to understand the action of the Board in permitting the publication of the inaccurate statements and injurious reflections contained in the *Official History*, and the subsequent refusal of the Admiralty to take steps to have the inaccurate statements corrected and the adverse comments based on those inaccurate statements deleted.

The prime minister has stated that the cost of the *Official History of the War* is defrayed out of public money. The public have, therefore, the right to demand some guarantee of the accuracy of that work, and a clear definition of the responsibility attaching to its authorship. As matters stand, the Ministerial and official statements on the subject are as follows:—

1. The book is entitled, outside, *Official History of the War*.

2. Inside, the Lords Commissioners of the Admiralty state that "they are in no way responsible" for the author's "reading or presentation of the facts as stated."

3. In his preface, the author, Sir Julian S. Corbett, states that "for the form and character of the narrative, as well as for opinions expressed, the author is alone responsible."

4. The First Lord of the Admiralty, on 18th February, 1920, stated in the House of Commons that the first volume of the Naval History of the war was "being compiled *under the directions* of the Committee of Imperial Defence."

5. The prime minister, on 1st November, 1920, stated in the House of Commons that Sir Julian Corbett was "responsible as author "to the Committee of Imperial Defence.

6. The Prime Minister, on 1st November, 1920, also stated in the House of Commons that Sir Julian Corbett "is writing the official account of the war *from the Admiralty point of view.*"

7. In the course of a letter appearing in the *Nineteenth Century and After* (November 1920), Sir Julian Corbett states that he submitted the proof of his work to the Admiralty, and that the proofs, "after careful examination" were "returned to me with a few suggestions as to the wording of certain passages."

To sum up. The book is official. It is not official. It is compiled under the directions of a Cabinet Committee. It is written from the point of view of the Admiralty. The proofs are submitted to the Admiralty and are altered by the Admiralty. The Admiralty are not responsible. The author is alone responsible.

★★★★★★

From Hansard (House of Commons), 23rd June, 1920.
Naval Operations of the War.

Mr. Lambert asked the First Lord of the Admiralty whether, in Volume 1 of *Naval Operations of the War*, Sir Julian Corbett had access to all the documents in the possession of the Admiralty relating to the events described; whether the proofs of this volume were submitted to, and approved of, by the Admiralty; and whether the Admiralty accepts responsibility for the statements contained in this history based on official documents?

Mr. Long: It will be sufficient for me to quote the statement which faces the title page of the volume, namely—

> The Lords Commissioners of the Admiralty have given the author access to official documents in the preparation of this work, but they are in no way responsible for his reading or presentation of the facts as stated.

The Admiralty saw the proofs and agreed to publication; but, as stated, do not accept responsibility."

It will be observed that, although Mr. Lambert asked if Sir Julian Corbett had access to "all" the documents, the First Lord in his reply mentioned "documents" only.

From Hansard (House of Commons), 15th December, 1920.
Battle of Jutland.

Sir J. Craig: All the material, including Captain Harper's record, will be placed at Sir Julian Corbett's disposal, and this undertaking will be interpreted in the widest possible way. The Admiralty have no control over the use which Sir Julian Corbett makes of his material, and, therefore, so far as they are concerned, it is open to him to publish the material in whatever form he thinks proper.

Rear-Admiral Adair: Will the right hon. gentleman say whether it is the case that, although this record is handed to Sir Julian Corbett, the Admiralty refuses all responsibility as to what he publishes?

Sir J. Craig: All we possess in regard to what I have enumerated will be handed to Sir Julian. We have no control over him after that.

Sir R. Hall: Will the book published by Sir Julian Corbett be regarded as the Official Naval History of the War?

Sir J. Craig: I am not quite certain of the terms under which Sir Julian was asked to write the history of the War. He was asked to do so by the Committee of Imperial Defence, and not by the Admiralty.

Viscount Curzon: Are the Admiralty going to allow these counter publications without any revision whatever? Can Sir Julian publish what he likes?

Sir J. Craig: I understand that the Committee of Imperial Defence, when it entered into the agreement, imposed certain conditions, but I am not quite sure what they are."

★★★★★★

The truth is, that the prime minister, having stated in Parliament that the *Official History of the War: Naval Operations*, Vol. 1, is written from the Admiralty point of view, the assertion that the comments in the book represent only the opinions of Sir Julian Corbett, is no longer tenable. Unless the prime minister's statement is contradicted as formally as it was made, the public are entitled to accept every statement in the book as authorised by the Board of Admiralty, and every comment thereon as expressing the views of the Board of Admiralty.

The author, Sir Julian S. Corbett, is at least responsible for omitting to consult the late commander-in-chief in the Mediterranean in respect of important events occurring under his command. While Sir Julian Corbett was preparing his material, I was entirely at his service, and I should have had much pleasure in giving him any assistance in my power. Sir Julian Corbett's statement, contained in his letter published in *The Nineteenth Century* (November 1920), that his narrative was "tested for accuracy of detail by senior officers who were engaged in the operations," is the more surprising. It was certainly never submitted to me *before* publication; and the results of the "testing for accuracy of detail" *after* publication appear in the foregoing pages. I have already said that, upon my discussing the matter with Sir Julian Corbett, he was unable to afford me any explanation or to suggest any redress.

Sir Julian Corbett also states in the same letter, that he "was given the freest possible access to the secret files which contain the telegrams that passed between the Admiralty and the admiral, as well as to the instructions. . ." It is therefore clear that although Sir Julian Corbett was cognisant of my instructions relating to war with Austria, in the passages of the *Official History*, in which he refers to my dispositions made at the time when I was informed that a state of war existed between Austria and Great Britain, those instructions, whether by inadvertence or design, were ignored by the historian.

It is equally clear that in this case, as in others, the Admiralty allowed a false implication to pass. If, in the judgment of the Admiralty, or of Sir Julian Corbett, or of both, it was inadvisable to state in what those instructions consisted, there can have been no indiscretion in stating either that they existed or that they were fulfilled. The absolute necessity of instantly fulfilling Admiralty orders concerning my dispositions in the event of war with Austria did, in fact, govern the whole situation. The consequent delay enabled the *Goeben* and *Breslau* to make good their retreat.

That the telegram announcing a state of war with Austria was despatched, was evidently an accident. Such accidents occur in war as in peace.

I have accurately narrated the course of events, and the public are now enabled to form a just estimate of the episode. It remains for the authorities to ensure that the *Official History of the War: Naval Operations* Vol. 1 is so corrected as to accord with the facts contained in the Admiralty records.

"Goeben" and "Breslau"—The Far East: Siege of Tsingtau

W. L. Wyllie & M. F. Wren

In the good old days when our men-o'-war still carried sails, when snowy decks and bright brasswork were considered much more important than gunnery; easy-going days when engines of 20,000 horsepower were spoken of with awe and wonder, and wireless messages or the submarine were yet undreamed of, the Mediterranean Fleet was a symbol of the power of Britain. All the newest creations of our best designers, the "*Alexandras*," "*Sultans*," "*Monarchs*," or "*Inflexibles*" of that time were sent out to serve a long commission under the famous Admirals who carried out the evolutions of their sea-monsters with such marvellous perfection.

The Mediterranean Fleet was sea-power personified. It could demolish a few miles of Egyptian forts, terrorise a coast line, or overawe refractory islanders in the Aegean. It held the communications between the Near and the Far East. After a gale, when its units had ridden with topmasts housed and lower yards on the hammock netting, the ships of the Mediterranean Fleet, when the signal was made to cross topgallant yards, would send the spars aloft and have everything ready to make all plain sail in fewer minutes than any other fleet. In it the rate of signalling was much faster, and the sailing and rowing regattas were the envy of all other squadrons.

With the rise of the German Navy our most powerful ships were, as time went on, ordered to join fleets nearer England. New names were invented, such as Atlantic and Home fleets, while the men-o'-war sent to show our flag and keep up our prestige in the Near East dwindled from year to year. The Liberal Governments had not built sufficiently to keep up our sea-power on all seas.

At the outbreak of the present war the fleet in the Mediterranean was composed as follows:

Three battle cruisers: *Inflexible* (flag of Admiral Sir Berkeley Milne), *Indomitable, Indefatigable*. Four cruisers: *Defence* (flag of Rear-Admiral Troubridge), *Warrior, Duke of Edinburgh, Black Prince*. Four light cruisers: *Chatham, Weymouth, Dublin, Gloucester*. One parent ship, *Blenheim*, and sixteen destroyers. One dispatch vessel: *Hussar*.

We had no Dreadnoughts or super-Dreadnoughts.

Vague rumours of European unrest had been floating about for some time, and officers on leave in Cairo and other places had been recalled; then, on July 28, 1914, the ships left Alexandria, steaming west. There were to have been practice night attacks by destroyers, but these were not carried out, the crews being exercised in war routine instead, sham fighting giving place to real. The ammunition for the 4-inch guns was brought up, and at midnight the speed of the ships was increased to twenty knots. The peace of Europe seemed in great danger. When Malta was reached on the 30th the fleet found the town seething with excitement; all the troops in the island had been mobilised. *Indomitable* was in dock; she had just started to refit, but she was brought out, and at once began taking in ammunition. All officers were warned of the importance of secrecy, both in letters and in conversation. There were plenty of German spies about, as indeed throughout the Empire.

All gear was to be landed. On Friday, the 31st, the news was serious: France and Russia were mobilising. The whole day was spent getting in provisions, ammunition, and fusing the lyddite shells. All bright work was painted over; even the priceless white enamel of *Hussar*, on which so much money and labour had been expended, was hurriedly daubed over with grey. Sea-boats were topped up into their fighting positions, and all the rest, except the boom-boats, were put ashore. The bulk of the craft put to sea on August 1. Those which remained darkened ship, sentries with loaded rifles were posted fore and aft, picket boats with armed crews patrolled the harbour, and the boom defence was put in position.

Black Prince, which was to have carried Lord Kitchener from Marseilles to Egypt, returned on the 3rd, for this great soldier had more important work to do in England. Martial law and a Moratorium were declared in Malta. There was news that Germany had declared war on Russia, and that the Cabinet was meeting in London to discuss the attitude of England. *Inflexible* left the Grand Harbour with all guns

THE ARMOURED CRUISER *DUBLIN*

loaded, hands at night defence stations, and ship darkened.

Next day it was known that the *Kaiser's* Government had asked Belgium's permission for troops to pass through her territory; that this had been refused, and that England had sent an ultimatum to Germany, which expired at midnight on the 4th. Captains of some of the ships gave interesting lectures on the European situation to their ships' companies. There were two fast German ships in these waters: *Goeben*, which carried ten 11-inch and twelve 6-inch guns, and could steam twenty-eight knots; and *Breslau* one of the "Town" class, armed with twelve 4-inch guns. They had been up the Adriatic, but were reported off Bizerta. The French were, at this moment, transporting the 19th Army Corps, a considerable number of troops, from Algeria and Tunis to help their Mother Country against threatened invasion.

On the 3rd there was war between France and Germany, and the fast German ships, making their appearance off Bona and Philippeville, bombarded those towns and steamed away.

It must be remembered that the problem set before the British Fleet was difficult in the extreme. We were not yet at war, but the transports of our friends the French had to be protected from attack by the German ships, which, though no match for our three battle cruisers, were, in consequence of their greater speed, able to choose their own object or moment for attack. No one knew where the stroke might fall, nor could guess that the real object of the *Kaiser's* Government was only to bring the two ships to Constantinople, where their presence might help Enver Pasha and the Young Turks' Party in their guilty plot to drag their country into the war which was seen to be impending.

Only six hours before war was declared, two of our battle cruisers, *Indomitable* and *Indefatigable*, actually met the two Germans cruising between Sicily and Sardinia. Our ships, steaming westward, passed within 2,000 yards of the *Goeben*, which was heading towards the Straits of Messina.

If only it had been possible to stop these two ships, the whole course of the war in the East might have been different. Turkey might never have entered the war, and there would have been peace in Armenia and Mesopotamia. We should have been spared the heartbreaking reports of prisoners' sufferings in Asia Minor, and the glorious but fatal expeditions to the Gallipoli Peninsula might never have happened.

Unfortunately, the ultimatum had not expired; therefore, our powerful ships could only turn and follow after their probable enemies, hoping for the moment when they could bring them to action.

The speed of *Goeben* and *Breslau*, however, was twenty-eight knots, and, steam as the British ships might, the distance gradually lengthened till the Germans became only puffs of smoke below the horizon. Course was therefore altered, *Indomitable* going to Bizerta to coal, while *Inflexible* and *Indefatigable* kept watch off the south-east of Sardinia, with steam for full speed at one hour's notice, hoping to waylay the *Goeben* if she had another try at the French transports.

At 1 45 a.m. on Wednesday, August 5, the expected signal was received by our ships in Mediterranean waters:

WAR DECLARED WITH GERMANY.

Chatham captured a German collier; first blood to us. On the 6th, not meeting the Germans, the two battle-cruisers became uneasy and steered towards the northern entrance of the Straits of Messina. *Indomitable* joined up shortly afterwards, and at dusk a message came from *Gloucester*, which was watching the southern entrance of the Straits, that *Goeben* and *Breslau* were coming out. A little later they were reported steering eastward.

At this moment the four cruisers, *Defence*, *Warrior*, *Duke of Edinburgh*, and *Black Prince*, were off Cephalonia, but *Dublin*, a light cruiser, was farther to the south, with two destroyers, and an order was sent to her to make a night attack on the enemy ships. Most unfortunately, the night was pitch dark, and, steering without lights, she missed them by a few miles. The plucky little *Gloucester* was still shadowing the two German cruisers, and now reported the enemy to be steering to the northward, running in the direction of Rear-Admiral Troubridge and his squadron. On the 7th the admiral reported that he had failed to find *Goeben* and *Breslau*.

The French admiral now signalled that he would finish convoying the troops from Africa on the 10th; so, the three battle cruisers, *Inflexible*, *Indomitable*, and *Indefatigable*, having coaled at Malta, once more starts in chase of the still elusive Germans. They were too slow to catch them, though in the meantime *Gloucester* had had a very long-range action with *Breslau*. *Goeben* tried to take part, but *Gloucester* withdrew out of range, still continuing to shadow the Germans until shortness of coal caused her recall.

The two German cruisers, henceforth undisturbed, rounded Cape Matapan and proceeded under easy steam up the Aegean Sea.

THE ARMOURED CRUISER *INFLEXIBLE*, (FLAG)

The battle cruisers, about fifty miles astern, searched the Greek islands without result. Next day an Italian tramp steamer reported that both our enemies were at anchor off Chanak, so speed was increased, and the Dardanelles were reached at 10 p.m. *Weymouth*, going in near the forts, was fired at with blank cartridge, and in the morning a Turkish officer, boarding the ship from the shore, informed the captain that *Goeben* and *Breslau* had been sold to Turkey. They were, however, still flying the German flag when they sent an armed party on board a Messageries Maritimes steamer in neutral waters and forced the crew to dismantle their wireless.

With the finish of the chase of *Goeben* and *Breslau*, our account of the doings of the Mediterranean Fleet comes to an end. Many of the ships composing it were sent to other seas.

In Mediterranean Waters

Charles Gill

COMPARISON OF FORCES AND ESTIMATE OF THE NAVAL SITUATION AT THE BEGINNING OF THE WAR

From the pre-war-time disposition of naval forces it is evident that the understanding between France and England in regard to naval operations in the middle sea assigned to the former the paramount duty of accounting for the enemy in the event of hostilities between the Triple Entente—Great Britain, France and Russia—on the one hand, and the Triple Alliance—Germany, Austria and Italy—on the other. Great Britain and Russia would be expected to furnish such assistance as circumstances might permit, but the responsibility for the control of the Mediterranean apparently rested on the shoulders of the French Chief Command.

At the beginning of the war. Admiral Lapeyrere was Commander-in-Chief of the French Fleet, and it is to be remembered that in the critical first days of August his problem was complicated by the fact that the attitude of Italy was uncertain. Immediately after the declaration of war between France and Germany on August 3, 1914, however, Italy declared her neutrality and this created a naval situation in the Mediterranean which gave the Allies an overwhelming superiority in ships and guns.

The French Fleet available for Mediterranean service consisted of four dreadnought battleships, twenty pre-dreadnought battleships, twenty-two armoured cruisers, nine light cruisers, eighty-four destroyers and sixty-four submarines. An approximate comparison of this fleet with the Austrian naval forces shows that the French Navy was: —

125

2½ times that of Austria in battleships.

8¾	"	"	"	armoured cruisers
3	"	"	"	protected cruisers
2½	"	"	"	destroyers.
3½	"	"	"	torpedo boats.
12	"	"	"	submarines.

In addition to the Austrian Fleet, a German squadron under command of Admiral Souchon, consisting of the battle cruiser *Goeben* and light cruiser *Breslau*, was cruising in the Mediterranean at this time. But, to more than counterbalance this, in reinforcement of the French Fleet, England had a squadron in these waters under the command of Admiral Milne, seconded by Admiral Troubridge, consisting of three battle cruisers, two armoured cruisers, three light cruisers, and a flotilla of destroyers. The particular mission of this British squadron seems to have been to capture or destroy the two German cruisers, but whether this was explicitly the case or not, it would hardly relieve the French commander-in-chief of his full share of responsibility for their subsequent escape.

An Aggressive Plan Lacking

Under the circumstances it would appear reasonable to have expected the superior Allied Fleets to conduct a vigorous offensive. A complete report is not available of just what occurred in the Mediterranean and for that reason comment should be offered with reservation, but it is certain that no positive results were obtained, and French and English naval forces, either by inaction or by misdirected action, failed to take advantage of an opportunity for performing services which might have had far-reaching effects upon the course of the war.

In the first place, it is not clear why more aggressive demonstrations were not made in the Adriatic against Austria by the Allied fleet. To be sure, the Austrian fleet was contained in this small sea while the Allies had free use of the Mediterranean, except for submarine depredations. But this could have been accomplished with less than half of the Allied naval force actually employed. A few excursions are reported to have been made in the Adriatic, but they had no important results and the enemy seems to have enjoyed almost unrestricted freedom in this sea to the southward as far as Cattaro.

Montenegro and Serbia were Allies, and Italy was disposed to be friendly. Under these circumstances a more aggressive strategy on the part of Allied naval power might have had beneficial consequences, especially in its influence upon wavering neutrals.

It has been argued, moreover, that Cattaro offered an objective of considerable promise for a combined land and sea attack. An attack was planned, but not being adequately supported either by land or by sea, it failed. Finally, the conquest of Montenegro and Serbia gave the enemy control of the eastern coast of the Adriatic. On this question of whether or not the Allies should have conducted a naval offensive in the Adriatic, however, there are two sides. Expert opinion was, and still is, divided as to the advisability of risking ships by advancing against an enemy fleet on the defensive, protected by mines and torpedoes. The circumstances and conditions peculiar to the special naval situation will determine the decision. More light is required before drawing definite conclusions respecting the conduct of the Adriatic naval campaign.

In the second place, and in this there is little difference of opinion, it is hard to understand how the *Goeben* and *Breslau* could have escaped if a proper disposition of the French and British ships had been promptly made. The Allies had in the Mediterranean at this time numerous men-of-war possessing both speed and power, including three British battle cruisers, several fast light cruisers, and many destroyers. Although the German force was a small one, and while at first glance its escape does not appear as a matter of very great consequence, in reality this episode had far-reaching political consequences, and points an important naval lesson.

"*GOEBEN*" AND "*BRESLAU*" ESCAPE

Just how the German Cruisers in the Mediterranean got away from the British explained from German sources.

Summary from an account published in Germany by Dr. Emile Ludewig.

In the latter part of July, 1914, the *Goeben* and the *Breslau* were in the Adriatic. The *Goeben*, under the command of Admiral Souchon, completed repairs at Pola on July 30th, and was then ready to go to sea.

The admiral decided, on account of the strained relations following the assassination of the Archduke of Austria, to move toward the Straits of Gibraltar and be in readiness to dash into the Atlantic on short notice if war became imminent and the German Government so ordered.

On August 1st the *Goeben* was joined by the *Breslau* at Brindisi. On August 2nd, the two ships sailed for Messina and coaled there. During the night of August 2nd, the squadron sailed to the westward.

On August 3rd, Admiral Souchon was informed by radio of the declaration of war between Germany and France, and also received instructions to go to Constantinople.

Being at this time in the neighbourhood of the Algerian coast, he decided to bombard Bona and Philippeville before proceeding to the east, hoping by this manoeuvre to confuse the enemy as to his real intentions. The *Goeben* bombarded Philippeville at 4.40 a. m., August 4th, while the *Breslau* conducted a simultaneous bombardment of Bona.

The two ships then rendezvoused at sea, heading to the north and west. At about fifty miles from Bona they sighted an English squadron, which followed them during the day, but was out-distanced in the evening. The speed of the German ships was 28 knots. After steering various courses to deceive the enemy as to their true destination, they headed for Sicily, and anchored at Messina at 5.00 p. m. on August 5th. Coal was obtained there with difficulty, as Italy refused to accede to their demand for replenishment.

In the afternoon of August 6th, an Italian officer, in the name of his government, invited them to leave the port of Messina. Admiral Souchon thereupon requisitioned the German liner General, which he found in this port, and directed her to leave port a short distance behind the two cruisers, and to follow them in the direction of Constantinople. On the same day the German admiral learned of the declaration of war between Germany and England, and was also informed that the entrances to Messina were guarded by English warships. At 5.00 p. m., the *Goeben* and *Breslau* sailed from Messina.

They were trailed by the English cruiser *Gloucester* at a distance of 20,000 meters. The German admiral did not open fire upon the *Gloucester*, nor did he interfere with the wireless messages she was sending to other cruisers.

At 10 o'clock that night, however, the weather having become overcast, Admiral Souchon ordered a radical change of course, and instead of continuing toward the Adriatic, he headed for Matapan. At the same time, he ordered the radio of the *Goeben* to jam the signals of the *Gloucester*. The *Gloucester* lost contact during the night, but regained it the next morning, August 7th, at 5. 00 a. m., and engaged the *Breslau* until threatened by the *Goeben*, when she withdrew.

On the 7th of August, Admiral Souchon received from Berlin a message informing him that entry to the Dardanelles at that time was

The Former German Cruiser *Goeben*

With her sister ship the *Breslau*, she escaped from the British Fleet in the Mediterranean, both ships making their way to Constantinople.

not possible. The two German cruisers then proceeded to the Isle of Denusa, where the liner *General* was directed to join them. The latter was first sent to Smyrna to ascertain the attitude of the Turks toward the German squadron.

On August 8th and 9th, the two cruisers found a collier and coaled at Denusa without molestation. Then, on the afternoon of the 9th, having received a message from Berlin informing them that the Turkish authorities were agreeably disposed, the German squadron proceeded to the Dardanelles. They anchored inside the Straits at Chanak, and a few hours later English cruisers arrived outside the entrance.

★★★★★★

It was rumoured that while off the northern coast of Africa the two German cruisers, when hard beset by enemy forces, escaped during misty weather by the aid of a ruse—that of placing some musicians on a raft to attract the attention of enemy patrols by playing German airs, while the warships laid their course for Messina.

★★★★★★

An explanation of the escape of these two ships from the Allied naval forces has not yet been given, but it would appear that either there was a proper plan lacking, or, if there was a proper plan, somebody blundered badly in putting it into execution. It must be that the French commander-in-chief was kept informed of the movements of the *Goeben* and *Breslau* from port to port. Certainly, they disclosed their position by bombarding Bona and Philippeville. It would be interesting to know what steps were taken. To block the Straits of Gibraltar would have been a simple matter.

It is assumed that at least a large part of the French Fleet was either at or close to Bizerta. With the forces available it would appear by no means difficult to bar effectively the passage between Sicily and Cape Bon. That the German admiral might head for Messina must have been foreseen. Later, when the ships were known to be in Messina, it would seem that dispositions could have been made by which they would have been compelled to engage superior forces. Finally, what were the Allied ships doing between August 6th and August 9th?

THE LOG OF THE *GOEBEN*

International law required that the German warships leave the neutral port of Messina within twenty-four hours. The chances for escape appeared dubious to say the least, and the following version of the manoeuvre, purporting to be based on the log of the *Goeben*, is of interest:

On Aug. 6, 1914, just before sailing from Messina the German commander issued these orders:
'News about the enemy is uncertain. I presume his strength lies in the Adriatic and that he is watching both exits to the Messina Strait. Our object is to break through to the east and reach the Dardanelles. I want to create the impression that we intend to go to the Adriatic. In case I so succeed I will veer round in the night and make for Cape Matapan, if possible, throwing the enemy off our track.'

As the ships—flags flying and music playing—were reaching the open sea the following wireless message from the *Kaiser* reached the admiral: 'His Majesty expects the *Goeben* and the *Breslau* to succeed in breaking through.'

Shortly after leaving the harbour the English cruiser *Gloucester* appeared on the horizon. The English cruiser was emitting signals in three groups. The word 'Mumfu' frequently occurred and it was clear that it referred to the *Goeben*. The wireless receivers interpreted the signal of the British cruiser as follows: '*Goeben* making for the Adriatic.'

The German wireless officer argued thus: 'I can jam him. If I break my waves against his perhaps, I can confuse, hold up, destroy his messages. Shall I jam his wireless?' he asked the admiral. 'Shall we fire?' asked the commander.

'No,' was the answer to both questions. No one apart from the staff understood the admiral. This is how he argued, however: 'This boat is evidently a patrol, intending to wireless our movements to the main British fleet. He shall save us, not ruin us. He shall do his work. We will neither fire at nor jam him. Let him wireless that the Germans are making for the Adriatic, whereas the Dardanelles is our object.'

It was dark. The *Breslau* closed in. It was 10 o'clock in the evening; then came the order from the bridge: 'Starboard; make for Cape Matapan.'

The watching British cruiser saw the manoeuvre, but before she could wireless the news that the Germans were making for the east the following order flashed out from the admiral: 'Jam the wireless; jam it like the devil.'

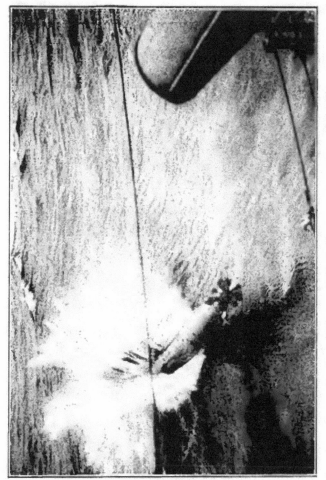

A Torpedo Taking the Water

For hours the Germans were travelling eastward without obstacle, while the patrol boat tried to make itself understood in vain. Where did the error of our enemy lie? In England the excuse was advanced that the Germans had acquired knowledge of the British secret wireless code and so deceived the latter into waiting. Is it worthwhile contradicting such stuff? The English should have waited before the Strait of Messina, and nowhere else. But so confident were they that the *Goeben* and *Breslau* must try and break through to the Adriatic in order to reach an Austrian port, that they thought it safe to wait in the Strait of Otranto, which is forty sea miles wide. So positive were they on this point that the thought of our making for the Dardanelles never seems to have occurred to them.

When the wireless messages of the *Gloucester* finally reached the British fleet, it was too late. The German ships were *en route* for Constantinople.

BOTH CRUISERS SOLD TO TURKEY

That this episode caused the Allies considerable chagrin may well be imagined. A little later, apparently as an alternative to disarming and being interned, the *Goeben* and *Breslau* were sold by Germany to Turkey, a transaction without precedent and involving a question of international law. Sharp representations were made by the Allies to Turkey, claiming that the latter had violated her neutrality and demanding immediate repatriation of the officers and crews. Turkey failed to comply with this demand and it is reasonable to suppose that the presence of the two warships in Constantinople had considerable influence in persuading the Turkish Government to join Germany and Austria in the war.

At this initial period in near-eastern affairs, determined action on the part of the Allies toward Turkey might possibly have had important effects.

Suppose, for example, that a powerful combined British and French naval force had steamed through the Dardanelles up to Constantinople and demanded the surrender of the *Goeben* and *Breslau* because of Turkey's alleged violation of neutrality laws. Suppose, also, if Turkey had forbidden this passage and refused these demands, that the Allied force had fought its way through the Dardanelles and either captured or destroyed the *Goeben* and *Breslau* in spite of any armed resistance which might have been afforded. It is, of course, problematical how much strength Turkey could have shown at this time, but it is not an unreasonable supposition that a resolute naval demonstration in the Dardanelles might have been successful and might have had a decisive influence on the wavering Turks, with consequently far-reaching effects upon the general course of the war.

Immediately upon the arrival of the *Goeben* and *Breslau*, Turkey, under the direction of German naval and military strategists, began to make ready for her entry into the war. The British Admiral Limpus and his staff, who had previously been employed to reorganise the Turkish Navy, were soon eliminated and superseded by a German admiral and German staff. A German liner previously employed in the East African trade arrived soon after the *Goeben*, having slipped through the Allied patrols. She carried a cargo of mines and other naval stores which were quickly put to use to guard the entrance to the Straits. At the same time heavy guns, munitions and other war stores were being imported across Rumania. From this time on, rapid progress was made in perfecting Turkish defences, preparatory to the war declaration of October 31, 1914.

★★★★★★

In some after-the-war articles widely published in the press. Lord Fisher of Kilverstone. the First Sea Lord of the British Admiralty, 1904-10, and recalled to that post in 1914, wrote as follows:

> Again, the *Goeben* and *Breslau*, which turned Turkey into an enemy, naturally escaped because the British battle cruisers that were in the Mediterranean were not used. If the great battle cruisers that were in the Mediterranean had gobbled up the *Goeben* and *Breslau*. as the *Invincible* afterward gobbled up their sister German ships at the Falklands, there would have been no Gallipoli and the Baltic would have been occupied and Berlin captured by Russians landing on the Pomeranian beach, safely covered by a British fleet.

Note—In the later operations in which the *Breslau* was sunk by mines, the *Goeben* also was mined and in returning to port in a damaged condition was run aground due to an error in navigation. The Turks succeeded, however, in hauling her off and she proceeded to Constantinople, where she was interned under the terms of the armistice. Although the *Goeben* was frequently reported as severely punished in Black Sea engagements it appears that she, in fact, suffered very little damage during the war.

★★★★★★

A Ballad of "The Gloster" & "The Goeben"

Maurice Hewlett

Come landsmen all and ladies,
And listen unto me
A-singing of the *Gloster*
Upon the Middle Sea.

The *Goeben* and the *Breslau*
They cruised th' Italian main;
No ship was there to stay them,
Their course was fair and plain.

But when the cruel guns open'd
Upon them from the shore,
From stem to stern they shiver'd.
Not being men of war.

Says *Goeben*, "Mate, it won't do;
This means there's war declared.
We'll find a place to hold two,
Leastways if we be spared.

"The strait it is no place for us
With all these beastly shells;
We'll out and seek the Turkish waters
And the Dardanelles.

"Their winds are not so boist'rous,
Their men are not so free,
And not so hard on poor sailors
Weary of the sea."

Just then the saucy *Gloster*
And her four thousand tons

Came up against the *Goeben*
And ran beneath her guns.

"What make you on the high sea,
And whither will you fare?"
"We seek a goodly haven
Where we can take the air."

"I'll send you to a haven
Which ought your case to fit.
D. Jones is harbour-master.
You show him this 'ere chit."

The seaman gunner pickt a shell
And spat upon it first;
Says he, "This here should give 'em beans,
If so be that she burst."

The *Breslau* gives a holloa,
"Be careful how you play;
For by your random marksmanship
My funnel's shot away."

"Good shooting," says the *Gloster*
"Now give the *Goeben* one."
And being on a stern chase
She lays the swivel gun.

A thirty shots the *Goeben*
Let fly; the *Gloster* three;
And one she raked the main deck.
And one she struck the sea;

The third she struck amidships.
"A-done!" the *Goeben* bawled;
"I've got a nasty list now,
And must be overhauled.

"But for that blasted *Gloster*—
If I could do her down
I'd be the brightest jewel
Upon my *Kaiser's* crown.

"She beats us with her gunning;
But we've got better heels.
Let's have a race," says *Goeben*
"And see how vict'ry feels."

The *Gloster* she gave over—
She'd had her little games.
The *Breslau* and the *Goeben*
They now bear other names.

Now God bless all our seamen
Who keep the English seas,
And send them equal fortune,
With worthier foes than these!

LEONAUR

ALSO FROM LEONAUR
AVAILABLE IN SOFTCOVER OR HARDCOVER WITH DUST JACKET

ESCAPE FROM THE FRENCH *by Edward Boys*—A Young Royal Navy Midshipman's Adventures During the Napoleonic War.

THE VOYAGE OF H.M.S. PANDORA *by Edward Edwards R. N. & George Hamilton, edited by Basil Thomson*—In Pursuit of the Mutineers of the Bounty in the South Seas—1790-1791.

MEDUSA *by J. B. Henry Savigny and Alexander Correard and Charlotte-Adélaïde Dard* —Narrative of a Voyage to Senegal in 1816 & The Sufferings of the Picard Family After the Shipwreck of the Medusa.

THE SEA WAR OF 1812 VOLUME 1 *by A. T. Mahan*—A History of the Maritime Conflict.

THE SEA WAR OF 1812 VOLUME 2 *by A. T. Mahan*—A History of the Maritime Conflict.

WETHERELL OF H. M. S. HUSSAR *by John Wetherell*—The Recollections of an Ordinary Seaman of the Royal Navy During the Napoleonic Wars.

THE NAVAL BRIGADE IN NATAL *by C. R. N. Burne*—With the Guns of H. M. S. Terrible & H. M. S. Tartar during the Boer War 1899-1900.

THE VOYAGE OF H. M. S. BOUNTY *by William Bligh*—The True Story of an 18th Century Voyage of Exploration and Mutiny.

SHIPWRECK! *by William Gilly*—The Royal Navy's Disasters at Sea 1793-1849.

KING'S CUTTERS AND SMUGGLERS: 1700-1855 *by E. Keble Chatterton*—A unique period of maritime history-from the beginning of the eighteenth to the middle of the nineteenth century when British seamen risked all to smuggle valuable goods from wool to tea and spirits from and to the Continent.

CONFEDERATE BLOCKADE RUNNER *by John Wilkinson*—The Personal Recollections of an Officer of the Confederate Navy.

NAVAL BATTLES OF THE NAPOLEONIC WARS *by W. H. Fitchett*—Cape St. Vincent, the Nile, Cadiz, Copenhagen, Trafalgar & Others.

PRISONERS OF THE RED DESERT *by R. S. Gwatkin-Williams*—The Adventures of the Crew of the Tara During the First World War.

U-BOAT WAR 1914-1918 *by James B. Connolly/Karl von Schenk*—Two Contrasting Accounts from Both Sides of the Conflict at Sea D uring the Great War.

CPSIA information can be obtained
at www.ICGtesting.com
Printed in the USA
BVHW040912140822
644459BV00016B/441